NEW PENGUIN SHAKESPEARE
GENERAL EDITOR: T. J. B. SPENCER
ASSOCIATE EDITOR: STANLEY WELLS

WILLIAM SHAKESPEARE

*

JULIUS CAESAR

EDITED BY
NORMAN SANDERS

PENGUIN BOOKS

PENGUIN BOOKS

Published by the Penguin Group
Penguin Books Ltd, 27 Wrights Lane, London W8 5TZ, England
Penguin Putnam Inc., 375 Hudson Street, New York, New York 10014, USA
Penguin Books Australia Ltd, Ringwood, Victoria, Australia
Penguin Books Canada Ltd, 10 Alcorn Avenue, Toronto, Ontario, Canada M4V 3B2
Penguin Books (NZ) Ltd, 182–190 Wairau Road, Auckland 10, New Zealand

Penguin Books Ltd, Registered Offices: Harmondsworth, Middlesex, England

This edition first published in Penguin Books 1967
Reprinted with a revised Further Reading 1996
3 5 7 9 10 8 6 4 2

Further Reading copyright © Michael Taylor, 1996

Set in Ehrhardt Monotype
Printed in England by Clays Ltd, St Ives plc

CONTENTS

INTRODUCTION

A SWISS doctor, Thomas Platter, visited London in 1599. During his stay in the city he saw two plays, and, when he came to write an account of his travels, he had this to say of one of them:

After lunch on September 21st, at about two o'clock, I and my party crossed the river, and there in the house with the thatched roof we saw an excellent performance of the tragedy of the first Emperor Julius Caesar with about fifteen characters; after the play, according to their custom they did a most elegant and curious dance, two dressed in men's clothes, and two in women's.

This play was almost certainly Shakespeare's *Julius Caesar*, which was therefore one of the first to be performed by Shakespeare's own Company, the Lord Chamberlain's Men, at their new theatre, The Globe, which they had had built on the Bankside in the early months of that year.

THE SUBJECT AND THE SOURCE

In turning to the fall of Julius Caesar and the conspiracy against him, Shakespeare was choosing to handle historical material which was not only well known, but had been for centuries a topic of interest and discussion; and one on which the Renaissance, with its urge to reassess the great historical figures of the past, had lavished particular attention in the form of prose and poetry, history and drama. In some ways, it was almost a natural subject to appeal to

7

a Shakespeare who had already written all of his major English history plays, with their national issues and complex political events seen in relationship to and growing out of the personalities and characters of those individuals who fashioned them.

As a busy man of the theatre and a working playwright, producing at least two plays a year, Shakespeare would almost certainly have been unable to spend his time reading widely in the standard works on the life and character of Caesar which had been published during the sixteenth century. And while there is evidence to suggest that he knew and was influenced by such works as the anonymous play, *Caesar's Revenge*, and a translation of Appian's *The Civil Wars* (1578), and even the verses on Caesar which had appeared in the 1578 edition of *A Mirror for Magistrates*, Shakespeare based his play almost totally on one of the most popular histories of the whole period. This work, *Plutarch's Lives of the Noble Grecians and Romans*, had been published in 1579 in the English translation of Sir Thomas North, who based his work not on the original Greek, but on the French version of Jacques Amyot which had appeared in 1559.

In fashioning his play, Shakespeare used three of Plutarch's Lives: *Marcus Brutus*, *Julius Caesar*, and *Marcus Antonius*. (References to North's Plutarch in the Introduction and Commentary of this edition are to *Shakespeare's Plutarch*, edited by T. J. B. Spencer (Penguin Books, 1964).) The accounts of the events immediately preceding Caesar's death and those subsequent to it are common to all three, with only the narrative spread, the focus, and some details being different. For the general shape of his plot, Shakespeare follows Plutarch's ordering of the narrative closely, using that Life which offered the most lively and striking description of the scene he wished to dramatize, while taking note of colourful or significant details in the others. Thus, for example, for the scenes at Philippi *Brutus* provides the most detailed descriptions of the battles fought and the deaths of Brutus and Cassius, so it is these Shakespeare draws on most heavily for his fifth Act; but he nevertheless incorporates some incidental remarks from *Caesar* and *Antonius*. At certain points he naturally compresses events which the narrative form permitted Plutarch to dwell on at length. He makes, for example, the Feast of the Lupercal and Caesar's Triumph for his victory over Pompey's sons, in fact separated by some four months, occur on the same day; he presents the two historical battles at Philippi as a single stage encounter in which the fortunes of the republican party are given a final test; and the murder of Caesar and Antony's incitement of the mob are the work of one day in the play instead of the two they occupy in the source. At other points, Shakespeare is content to dramatize almost without addition Plutarch's prose account, so that a single paragraph on the death of Cinna the poet or on the petition of Artemidorus becomes a short scene. At still others, where Plutarch offers only a hint of what was, for Shakespeare's purposes, an important dramatic event, he fashions a scene from his own imagination – as he does with the funeral of Caesar, where his source only offered him a few sentences about Brutus's and Antony's styles of oratory and about the effects their speeches produced on the Roman populace.

But North's translation offered the dramatist more than a plot and the subject matter for his scenes. Of the main characters – Caesar, Brutus, Antony, Cassius – the source contains fully-rounded portraits which preserve a nice balance between intimate personal detail and the role played by these men as political forces. Certainly Shakespeare adopts many features from these portraits. For example, the Cassius of the play is every bit as personally hysterical and politically acute as he is in Plutarch; but Shakespeare also introduces a warmth and desire for friendship into his nature which are lacking in the prose account. With Caesar too, he was able to capture the combination of man and 'Worthy' that Plutarch depicts; but he intensifies this complexity by focusing the audience's attention upon far more starkly contrasted extremes of personal weakness and superhuman claims. Brutus's idealistic and selfless devotion to his cause are as clear in the play as they are in the source, but in the former his gentleness is made a more positive and personal quality, and his idealism is tinged with an unattractive self-righteousness.

That Shakespeare admired North's prose style is also abundantly clear from the play. Its very unmetaphorical clarity suited well the 'plain' style that Shakespeare fashioned for his piece; so that at certain points he was able to take over some of North's lines almost unchanged to put into his characters' mouths. Thus North's 'Brutus did condemn and note Lucius Pella' becomes Shakespeare's 'You have condemned and noted Lucius Pella'; and Antony's laudation of Lucilius:

> *This is not Brutus, friend; but, I assure you,*
> *A prize no less in worth. Keep this man safe;*
> *Give him all kindness. I had rather have*
> *Such men my friends than enemies.*　　　　V.4.26–9

is closely based on North's prose:

> *But, I do assure you, you have taken a better booty than*
> *that you followed. For, instead of an enemy, you have*
> *brought me a friend. . . . For I had rather have such men*
> *my friends as this man here, than enemies.*
>
> 　　　　　　　　　　　　　　　　　　Brutus, page 169

Yet, even after Shakespeare's debt to North and Plutarch is detailed, what remains and what was changed is amply sufficient to make the play far more than a mere dramatization. The supremely well-proportioned plot is Shakespeare's own, from its opening on the celebration of a thriving city which has just emerged from a civil war, through the gradual knitting of the conspiracy, to the climax of the double defeat in Act III, and on to the rapid events of the second civil strife, the divisions and bickering in both parties, and the finale of victory and defeat, death and tribute. Among the characters also, Shakespeare created more than he borrowed: the Antony emerging in Act III is a unique complex creation interwoven from dedicated friendship, grief, and political opportunism; Casca, about whom Plutarch has only a handful of observations, comes to life in the play as a character as skilfully observed and psychologically credible as any minor figure in the Shakespeare canon; and the portraits of Calphurnia, Portia, and Cicero are convincing characterizations in a small compass created by Shakespeare out of the few actions which Plutarch records them as performing. With the style of the play too, the texture is Shakespeare's. For while its uncharacteristic lack of metaphorical richness makes it to some extent similar to North's direct strong prose, its variety is Shakespearian: the structural clarity of single lines and speeches is juxtaposed with the sudden vividly pictured metaphor – of the conspirators fawning round Caesar like hounds at the moment before death, or of Brutus's vision of Caesar as an emerging adder.

Shakespeare was able to count on the fascination which the character of Caesar had exercised since his own lifetime to provide his play with a kind of pre-performance appeal. But with this advantage he received both the enigma Caesar was and, more important, a tradition in which the judgements to which his character and death had given rise differed according to the political beliefs of their possessors. Generally speaking, the attitudes to the man and his end were, on the one hand, those which deplored the assassination of a man who personified a stable political order that, despite its weaknesses, had (for Elizabethans especially) the cardinal virtue of being stable; and, on the other hand, those which saw in the death of Caesar the timely elimination of a potential or already fully fledged tyrant. Both of these views had, for Shakespeare's audience, the most important implications concerning matters of government and right rule. But for Shakespeare himself, who had lately completed a long series of plays dealing with just these topics in terms of hereditary monarchy, they provided an opportunity to explore the very essence of his subject in a context which was less immediate than the doings of the Houses of York and Lancaster and the monarchs they produced, whose heir was drawing to the end of her long reign at the time of the play's writing.

CAESAR AND BRUTUS

Shakespeare's dramatic characterization of Caesar displays all of the contradictions associated with its historical original to such an extent that critics of the play have been plagued with them ever since. Caesar can easily be viewed as a man who has begun to believe in and live through his own legend, while being ironically afflicted with his share of human ills. There does exist the public figure who struts and preens himself in front of the Roman crowd, and pushes aside a genuine warning from the Soothsayer with the grand histrionic gesture and the assumed ability to read the mind's construction in the face:

> *Set him before me; let me see his face. . . .*
> *He is a dreamer. Let us leave him. Pass.* I.2.20, 24

There is too the confident ruler who falls readily, both publicly and in his own home, into the third person in speaking of himself, thereby creating an artificial distance between other mortals and himself. At one with this aspect of Caesar is his contemptuous arrogance (II.2.65–8) to the highest officers of the empire he heads:

> *Shall Caesar send a lie?*
> *Have I in conquest stretched mine arm so far,*
> *To be afeard to tell greybeards the truth?*
> *Decius, go tell them Caesar will not come.*

He assumes both god-like powers of resolution and the constancy of a natural force:

> *If I could pray to move, prayers would move me;*
> *But I am constant as the northern star,*
> *Of whose true-fixed and resting quality*
> *There is no fellow in the firmament. . . .*
> *Hence! Wilt thou lift up Olympus?* III.1.59–62, 74

It is true also that Shakespeare juxtaposes such pretensions as these, which we see enacted in the person of Caesar, with those very human and physical weaknesses that we hear from the lips of other characters: from Decius Brutus, that Caesar is 'superstitious grown of late'; from Cassius, that there was a time when his pride led him to accept a swimming-challenge which was beyond his powers; and from Casca, that his excitement in a political crisis induced a fit of epilepsy. Those who would like to see Shakespeare uncharacteristically simple in his methods support with this evidence their contention that the Caesar of the play is indeed merely a tyrannical wolf plaguing the Roman sheep.

Yet the total impression of Caesar gained from the play (rather than from selected passages from it) is far more complex. For the Caesar who is recovering from his fit in the second scene is also the acute observer of men and their natures; he sums up in a few lines the Cassius the audience has just witnessed – a man of personal envy, conscious superiority, and rigid political doctrine:

> *Yond Cassius has a lean and hungry look;*
> *He thinks too much: such men are dangerous. . . .*
> *He is a great observer, and he looks*
> *Quite through the deeds of men. . . .*
> *Seldom he smiles, and smiles in such a sort*
> *As if he mocked himself, and scorned his spirit*
> *That could be moved to smile at anything.*
> *Such men as he be never at heart's ease*
> *Whiles they behold a greater than themselves,*
> *And therefore are they very dangerous.*
>
> I.2.193–4, 201–2, 204–9

This is the political Caesar who can manage the Roman crowd by indulging the ritualistic refusal of the crown which it demands of him, even when such behaviour cuts counter to his own ambitions. This display of insight allows us to glimpse the man who, in the words of his friends, has never allowed his affections to sway more than his reason, in order to become the foremost man of all the world; and, in the words of his enemies, bestrides the world 'like a Colossus' and soars 'above the view of men' to become a god.

What Shakespeare has done in creating his Caesar is to spin the threads which go to make up the warp and woof of human personality, accepting all the seeming contradictions. In each of Caesar's own speeches and in those made by other characters about him, Shakespeare manages to suggest both the greatness and weakness, a fear and a show of courage, an unacknowledged doubt and a public assertion of consistency. Such contradiction is obvious in his perception of the danger represented by Cassius in the lines quoted above, and in his sudden resumption of his Caesarian role with the words:

> *I rather tell thee what is to be feared*
> *Than what I fear; for always I am Caesar.*　I.2.210–11

But it is present also in his fatalistic acceptance of death:

> *Cowards die many times before their deaths;*
> *The valiant never taste of death but once.*
> *Of all the wonders that I yet have heard,*
> *It seems to me most strange that men should fear,*
> *Seeing that death, a necessary end,*
> *Will come when it will come.*　　　　　II.2.32–7

Here is the wisdom of a true recognition of human limitation, combined with the regret that such must be; but the same man is to be led to comfort himself only a few lines later with the ironical brag that

> *Danger knows full well*
> *That Caesar is more dangerous than he.*　II.2.44–5

Each reader of the play can detect, with Brutus, those hints and clear indications that Caesar has grown so great as to constitute a threat of tyranny; but if he is to be faithful to the play Shakespeare wrote, then he must also admit the exceptional qualities of the man which come through – both in his own words and in the words of others. Each of these aspects is deeply written into the play, and both are overlaid throughout the early Acts by a sense of destiny controlled by those Fates which, in the words of Artemidorus, 'with traitors do contrive'.

Although Caesar is the titular hero of the play, and indeed central to its main issue, it is Brutus on whose decision this issue depends, and who is thus as near to being a tragic protagonist as any of the characters in a play which lacks a true central character in the usual sense. Brutus's action in making the conspiracy a reality had, like Caesar's character itself, been submitted, in the European tradition, to opposite interpretations. At one extreme, we have the medieval Brutus condemned to suffer at the centre of Dante's Inferno as a man guilty of criminal assassination and personal betrayal; and at the other, 'the noblest Roman of them all', Plutarch's 'angel', the one just man, gentle and altruistic, among the wicked and envious conspirators. As in the case of Caesar, both views can be supported by reference to the play. It is obvious, for example, that Shakespeare deliberately emphasized by specific incidents those 'gentle' elements in the character that Plutarch repeatedly claims for him. Only he among the conspirators is seen in circumstances and relationships which are but marginally related to the conspiracy itself. First, the scene with Portia shows his capacity for giving and inspiring deep and genuine affection:

> *You are my true and honourable wife,*
> *As dear to me as are the ruddy drops*
> *That visit my sad heart.* II.1.288–90

Secondly, in two short scenes with his boy, Lucius, regretful solicitude and a perceptiveness of innocence and its power permeate his lines. In public terms, too, the 'noble Brutus' is conveyed. Those who need his support for political purposes seem naturally to denigrate their own motives and actions in comparison with his; Casca expresses their attitude when he says:

> *O, he sits high in all the people's hearts;*
> *And that which would appear offence in us,*
> *His countenance, like richest alchemy,*
> *Will change to virtue and to worthiness.*   I.3.157–60

Cassius also allows that it is indeed 'noble mettle' in Brutus which he hopes 'may be wrought | From that it is disposed'; and Antony gives memorable and final testimony in his spoken epitaph at the end of the play:

> *He only, in a general honest thought*
> *And common good to all, made one of them.*
> *His life was gentle, and the elements*
> *So mixed in him, that Nature might stand up*
> *And say to all the world, 'This was a man!'*   V.5.71–5

But far more than any outside comment, Brutus himself makes his own impact directly on the audience; for, while to the other conspirators Caesar's death is but a plan to be made practicable, to him alone is it a moral issue which, set against his instinctive inclinations, can only be justified in terms of the greater value of public institutions, and which entails an inner debate which leaves its marks upon his whole nature.

It has, however, also been frequently pointed out that Brutus's nature contains, in addition, qualities which are neither noble, nor even humanly attractive. Alongside irreproachable personal integrity is an egoism which drives him to impose his will on his partners; after listening to Cassius on the conduct of the battle at Philippi, he prefers his own views with the brief, flat, 'Good reasons must perforce give place to better.' Similarly, dedicated to the public good, he is for ever aware of the historical and political value of his name and of his high reputation. He is consciously aware of his own moral rectitude:

> *There is no terror, Cassius, in your threats;*
> *For I am armed so strong in honesty*
> *That they pass by me as the idle wind,*
> *Which I respect not.*   IV.3.66–9

While it is true also that only Brutus of the plotters has a conscience, which makes him consider the implications of his deed, his judgement is consistently faulty once his decision to act has been taken. And it is his idealism that leads him to impose on the more politically realistic Cassius both a wrong policy concerning the treatment of Antony before the murder, and stagy impracticalities and further errors after it. Of the scenes depicting Brutus in his private character, it is noticeable that those with Portia and Lucius are preceded by others in which he is not seen to advantage. For example, one cannot withhold sympathy from the Brutus we see in his tent at the end of Act IV, as we watch him think of the comfort of his guards, search for his book, graciously ask for some music from his page, and then tolerantly display kind understanding of the boy's weakness. Nevertheless, immediately prior to all of this, we have witnessed another Brutus in his quarrel with Cassius, as arrogant as Caesar at his most arrogant, a man who sees himself as different from and superior to other men, and of whom Cassius can say truthfully:

> *A friend should bear his friend's infirmities;*
> *But Brutus makes mine greater than they are.*   IV.3.85–6

As in the case of Caesar, those critics of the play who have seized upon one or other of these different aspects of Brutus's character have done violence to Shakespeare's creation by making it simpler than it is. The Brutus of the play is neither purely the noble hero nor a blundering and unworldly idealist led by trickery. It is essential to the design of the play that he possess those qualities which the other conspirators lack, and which they need to make the assassination an actuality; but it is equally necessary that his mind be divided, that he be a bad judge of character, that he have a capacity for self-deception, and that his end be one filled with both tragic disillusion and unshaken conviction in his own rightness. However, the puzzle of Brutus is more dramatically significant than the enigma of Caesar, for on it depends how one views the achievement of the whole play – even what kind of play one takes it to be. But before taking up this difficulty, it is necessary to examine those aspects of the play about which there is fairly general agreement.

THE ACTION OF THE PLAY

Whatever else *Julius Caesar* is, it presents one of Shakespeare's most profound explorations of political action, viewed, as such action must always be, in close connexion with the characters of the men who perform it, and in relationship to the wider subject of morality itself. At the opening of the play the city of Rome and its people are engaged in a celebration of Caesar's victory in a civil war. As one part of the play is to be devoted to further civil strife, the scene thus anticipates, and also provides a wider historical context for, those events which are to take the centre of the stage. It prepares us in another way also, for, with the appearance of the two Tribunes, Flavius and Marullus, one possible source of antagonism to Caesar is revealed: that from the remaining supporters of Pompey the Great whose sons Caesar has just overcome. These men are seen to pay negative tribute to Caesar's supremacy by manipulating for their own political ends the crowd's acceptance of Caesar.

Immediately, Caesar's legendary eminence is shown quickly in his own brief commands, and in the almost obsequious obedience of those surrounding him:

ANTONY
When Caesar says, 'Do this', it is performed. . . .   I.2.10

CASCA
Peace, ho! Caesar speaks. . . .   I.2.1
Bid every noise be still; peace yet again!   I.2.14

CASSIUS
Fellow, come from the throng; look upon Caesar.   I.2.21

Whatever may be read into Caesar's lines on this appearance in the light of our subsequent knowledge of him, in terms of the stage the evidence of this scene does not point clearly to anything other than a powerful public man whose authority is accepted by himself and all those present. And this is all that is necessary at this point, for it is not with Caesar that the initiative for political action lies, but rather with his enemies; and it is these, Brutus and Cassius, that Shakespeare brings into dramatic focus.

THE CONSPIRACY

To group Brutus and Cassius together merely as 'conspirators' or 'enemies of Caesar' is to oversimplify the nature of the conspiracy, because they are different in character, motive, and intention. For Cassius, the drive to murder Caesar is deeply written into his very nature. Caesar's description of his character quoted above is as accurate as can reasonably be expected within its small compass. As an 'unharmonious' man 'who loves no music', Cassius is branded as a figure of disorder on both the personal and political levels. Personally, his hatred of Caesar is grounded in envy at beholding a greater than himself; and politically, his abhorrence is based on his belief in a free, republican Rome whose wide walls should encompass more than a single man. Neither of these emotions need necessarily lead a man to political action; but Cassius also has a philosophy that is more Renaissance than Roman, and which, to Shakespeare's original audience, was personified by the imperfectly-known but notorious figure of Nicolai Machiavelli: this is the concept of man as master of his own destiny independent of any superhuman power:

> Men at some time are masters of their fates;
> The fault, dear Brutus, is not in our stars,
> But in ourselves, that we are underlings.   I.2.138–40

It is this combination of the hate-infested man and the convinced republican, who, in Plutarch's words, 'even from his cradle could not abide any manner of tyrants', who attempts to seduce Brutus to his party. As he does so, the two basic strains in his nature intertwine. On the one hand, he is totally sincere in his belief that he

> had as lief not be as live to be
> In awe of such a thing as I myself   I.2.95–6

because he was 'born as free as Caesar'. But he speaks of these beliefs in a context that devalues them. For he slips constantly from his high standards of republicanism into a more material and personal support of them. Caesar's pretensions certainly violate Cassius's ideals, but the physical limitations of Caesar in comparison with the personal standards Cassius sets are more immediately influential. Thus his own daring challenge of the elements and of Caesar is set against Caesar's weak response:

> *Accoutrèd as I was, I plungèd in*
> *And bade him follow; so indeed he did.*
> *The torrent roared, and we did buffet it*
> *With lusty sinews, throwing it aside*
> *And stemming it with hearts of controversy.*
> *But ere we could arrive the point proposed,*
> *Caesar cried, 'Help me, Cassius, or I sink!'* I.2.105–11

It is this illustration that is brought forward to prove his point about individual freedom. Similarly, it is Caesar's fever in Spain which is used to show the human weaknesses of the eye 'whose bend doth awe the world', and of the tongue 'that bade the Romans | Mark him and write his speeches in their books'. In the Cassius who speaks of greatness in terms of feeding, and of honour in terms of personal achievement, we have the man whose political grasp is limited to immediate practice, whose mind cannot grasp abstract concepts, who can only perceive those standards which he himself creates, and for whom politics is the realm of personal relationships in which he is naturally inept, yet in which he craves success.

It is the function of this man to persuade Brutus, who is his opposite in almost every respect, to join the conspiracy. Although, because of his egotism, he is unfitted for the role of tempter, he is successful owing to the nature of the man he tempts. For, though Brutus is able without effort to inspire friendship and form close personal relationships, and has a mind which moves easily in the world of ideals and abstractions, he is unable to 'look quite through the deeds of men'. Throughout the scene between them, he is so wrapped in his own thoughts and fears about Caesar that he only half-listens to Cassius's words, or rather registers only those among them that are directly connected with his own misgivings. Over-conscious of his own heritage and the historical associations of his name, he quickly responds to Cassius's calculated weighing of this name with Caesar's:

> *Brutus and Caesar. What should be in that 'Caesar'?*
> *Why should that name be sounded more than yours?*
> *Write them together, yours is as fair a name;*
> *Sound them, it doth become the mouth as well;*
> *Weigh them, it is as heavy; conjure with 'em,*
> *'Brutus' will start a spirit as soon as 'Caesar'.*   I.2.141–6

With the sound of the crowd hailing Caesar offstage, he talks to Cassius of his beliefs in generalizing, abstract terms not in those of the immediate situation:

> *If it be aught toward the general good,*
> *Set honour in one eye, and death i'th'other,*
> *And I will look on both indifferently....*
> *Brutus had rather be a villager*
> *Than to repute himself a son of Rome*
> *Under these hard conditions as this time*
> *Is like to lay upon us.*   I.2.85–7, 171–4

It is due to these qualities in Brutus and to his fatal capacity for taking the name of a thing for the thing itself, or the utterance of a principle as proof of its existence, that Cassius is able to twist his 'honourable mettle'. In Cassius's soliloquy at the end of Act I, scene 2, we have a clear if limited statement of what we are to witness in the person of Brutus: namely, that qualities noble in themselves can be manipulated for less noble ends. In showing how he has used the friendship he longs for and himself professes to further a plan motivated primarily by personal envy, Cassius reveals the real nature of the conspiracy, which relies for its success on the conscious recognition that

> *it is meet*
> *That noble minds keep ever with their likes;*
> *For who so firm that cannot be seduced?* I.2.307–9

It should be noted, however, that owing to the ambiguous nature of the phrasing of some lines in this soliloquy, a different interpretation may be placed upon it. Many critics of the play have argued that, in this speech, Cassius is referring not to his own practice on Brutus, which we have just witnessed, but to Caesar's possible seduction of Brutus by favours and tyrannical influence. The evidence most frequently cited in support of this reading, however, comes not from the play itself, except indirectly, but from a passage in Plutarch which records how Cassius and his friends attempted to draw Brutus out of his relationship with Caesar and

> *prayed him to beware of Caesar's sweet enticements and to fly his tyrannical favours; the which they said Caesar gave him, not to honour his virtue but to weaken his constant mind, framing it to the bent of his bow.*
>
> *Brutus*, page 108

While it is impossible to prove that such an interpretation as this is wrong, it is nevertheless improbable, both because it depends on an awkward grammatical construction which, in the theatre, would almost certainly not convey the meaning required, and because it relies on a knowledge of material not contained in the play (an un-Shakespearian dramatic practice).

Despite the influence that Cassius can bring to bear on Brutus, both in personal encounter and by his device of planting forged letters purporting to represent the will of the Roman people, the decision which is to make the conspiracy a political fact rests with Brutus alone. It is for this reason that Shakespeare shows us only him in self-communication: for the decision must be seen to come out of his character. The speech recording this decision at the beginning of Act II is the crux of the play, and it has given rise to various and opposite interpretations. By this point, we are aware of what Brutus is, and, in the speech, all the tension between his nature and commitment to an action which violates this nature is obvious. Shakespeare is here trying to make credible simultaneously a man's determination to follow a course which, in terms of his character, is perverted, and those flaws and strengths in him which make such a perversion possible. But the degree of guilt we are meant to receive from the speech, and its implications for how we view Brutus, are variable. As the lines stand, Brutus misapplies logic wilfully, if unconsciously, and consequently decides on the basis of supposition and possibility, rather than on the proven evidence which points in the opposite direction. Although he admits that

> to speak truth of Caesar,
> I have not known when his affections swayed
> More than his reason . . .   II.1.19–21

yet he chooses to take the common proof over the particular instance and

> since the quarrel
> Will bear no colour for the thing he is,
> Fashion it thus: that what he is, augmented,
> Would run to these and these extremities;
> And therefore think him as a serpent's egg
> Which, hatched, would, as his kind, grow mischievous,
> And kill him in the shell.   II.1.28–34

The degree to which one sympathizes with or blames Brutus at this moment depends upon one's over-all view

of the play; but what is indisputable is that with Brutus's
attempt to resolve, by whatever means, what is essentially
a personal conflict with national implications, Shakespeare
links other signs of disorder. The very words Brutus uses
immediately following his moment of resolution convey
the nature of the insurrection his whole being is under-
going, even as the state of Rome will as a result of it:

> Between the acting of a dreadful thing
> And the first motion, all the interim is
> Like a phantasma or a hideous dream:
> The genius and the mortal instruments
> Are then in council; and the state of man,
> Like to a little kingdom, suffers then
> The nature of an insurrection.   II.1.63-9

This inward 'civil war' is that which is to produce its
outward counterpart in the final scenes of the play; but it
is also to have a more immediate correspondence in the
warring elements and prodigies that are described by Casca
in Act I, scene 3, and by Calphurnia in Act II, scene 2.
These monstrous and unnatural happenings in the natural
world were easily related by the Elizabethans both to man's
inner life and to society itself, owing to the infinite series
of interlocking correspondences which they perceived between the personal, social, material, and universal levels
of life. For Casca,

> When these prodigies
> Do so conjointly meet, let not men say,
> 'These are their reasons, they are natural';
> For, I believe, they are portentous things
> Unto the climate that they point upon.   I.3.28-32

Cassius on the other hand sees it as a 'very pleasing night
to honest men' which projects his own disordered state,

and presents him with a challenge to test the will of the gods by placing himself 'even in the aim and very flash' of the 'cross blue lightning'.

How one interprets these phenomena in the play is in accordance with one's point of view; as Cicero rightly notes,

> *men may construe things after their fashion,*
> *Clean from the purpose of the things themselves.* I.3.34-5

These unnatural happenings are connected with Caesar, and the disorder his tyranny creates in the body politic; but they also reflect the unnatural nature of the conspiracy against him, because 'The heavens themselves blaze forth the death of princes'. Both interpretations are voiced in the play, and Shakespeare pointed clearly to neither as being the right one. The final decision on this, as on so many other issues in the play, lies somewhere between Antony's laudation of Brutus and Brutus's own final lines on the futility of his action, between Caesar the man and Caesar the spirit.

Once Brutus has made the conspiracy possible by joining it, Shakespeare focuses on Brutus's recognition of the unpleasant aspects of the undertaking to which he is committed, and on his efforts to bring those things he perceives into line with the exalted motives he believes to be prompting him. In meeting his fellow conspirators as they skulk into his house muffled in their cloaks in the dead of night, he defines the nature of what he has decided to do:

> *O conspiracy,*
> *Sham'st thou to show thy dangerous brow by night,*
> *When evils are most free? O then, by day*
> *Where wilt thou find a cavern dark enough*
> *To mask thy monstrous visage?* II.1.77-81

As they confer at Brutus's house, the uneasy alliance of different personalities which the conspiracy really is begins also to emerge. What has been seen, up to this point, to be a balanced combination of the emotional drive and practicality of Cassius, and the necessary idealism of Brutus, turns out to have its own tensions. The price that Cassius has to pay for the plot's success is agreement to all of Brutus's errors of policy. The oath he proposes to bind them together is dismissed with an idealistic tirade by Brutus; and his advocacy of the need for Antony's death, as well as Caesar's, is denied as being butchery introduced into a sacrifice. Both of these decisions certainly grow out of those qualities which made Brutus's part in the conspiracy a necessity; but, more than this, they are a product of a Brutus who is now unconsciously trying to fit the violent means of the deed into his exalted vision of what the end will achieve. Thus an oath cannot be allowed, because they must not stain

> *The even virtue of our enterprise,*
> *Nor th'insuppressive mettle of our spirits,*
> *To think that or our cause or our performance*
> *Did need an oath; when every drop of blood*
> *That every Roman bears, and nobly bears,*
> *Is guilty of a several bastardy,*
> *If he do break the smallest particle*
> *Of any promise that hath passed from him.* II.1.133-40

And Antony's death would introduce a sacrilegious note into what he visualizes as a religious ceremony in which the body must suffer for the spirit's sake:

> *Let us be sacrificers, but not butchers, Caius.*
> *We all stand up against the spirit of Caesar,*
> *And in the spirit of men there is no blood.*

O, that we then could come by Caesar's spirit,
And not dismember Caesar! But, alas,
Caesar must bleed for it. And, gentle friends,
Let's kill him boldly, but not wrathfully;
Let's carve him as a dish fit for the gods,
Not hew him as a carcass fit for hounds.   II.1.166–74

During the course of this scene, Brutus's image has been tarnished to some degree. Each member of the audience must perceive the distance between Brutus's vision and the actuality of the deed he contemplates. And Shakespeare introduces two short encounters which, in part, elevate him to his early eminence above the other conspirators. In the first, Portia serves to remind us of the cost of Brutus's decision and the degree to which it affects his whole being as she describes, from the knowledge of intimacy, the past weeks:

It will not let you eat, nor talk, nor sleep;
And could it work so much upon your shape,
As it hath much prevailed on your condition,
I should not know you Brutus.   II.1.252–5

In the second scene, Caius Ligarius rises from his sick bed at Brutus's bidding, and, conjured by the magic of his name, is ready to follow

To do I know not what; but it sufficeth
That Brutus leads me on.   II.1.333–4

Yet, even though both these exchanges bring sympathy for Brutus, since they show us the trust and friendship and the love and devotion he can command, they simultaneously remind us by suggestion of other qualities. For Portia echoes her husband's awareness of his position, in her own pride in being Cato's daughter and 'the woman that Lord Brutus took to wife'; and she reflects also his

29

blurring of the necessity for physical violence and the proving an ideal, as she shows him the gash in her thigh, self-inflicted to test her constancy. With Caius Ligarius, too, sickness touches the conspiracy: Caesar must be 'made sick', so a sick man is healthy and will join the plot, if Brutus 'have in hand | Any exploit worthy the name of honour'.

THE ASSASSINATION AND THE FUNERAL

Just prior to the murder, Shakespeare allows us two glimpses of Caesar which in part confirm the fears Brutus has expressed. The arrogance and self-elevation, the posturing and thrasonical assertion are here more obvious than before. The strained impersonality of his relationship with his wife, Calphurnia, is purposely contrasted by Shakespeare with the tenderness and affection between Portia and Brutus which has just been witnessed. There is, too, a contradiction between his avowals of constancy and fatality, or the denial that danger does not exist for him, and his wavering indecision under the external pressures exerted by Decius Brutus and Calphurnia. Even after we have been allowed a sight of the gracious Caesar taking wine with his murderers, the alienation of sympathy towards him is built up by Shakespeare until the moment he is struck down as he stands, still asserting his superhuman 'fixity', which is to be disproved by the view of him as very much a man of flesh and blood, falling on Brutus's sword.

Before the murder has actually been committed, all other considerations and decisions made by the conspirators seem to be of subsidiary importance; but those actions they perform in its aftermath are of prime significance in their results. It is immediately after Caesar has died that the conspiracy displays a lack of direction. At this point,

the supernatural disorder of the previous night is given a
human and social counterpart in the description of the city
where

> *Men, wives, and children stare, cry out, and run,*
> *As it were doomsday.*   III.1.97–8

Some of the group share this hysteria, as Cinna and Cassius
call for 'Liberty, freedom, and enfranchisement' to be pro-
claimed through the streets and in the common pulpits.
Only Brutus has the calm necessary to reassure the aged
senator, Publius; and this calm is based on his ability to
keep in the forefront of his mind the abstract concept that
the deed represents: namely, that 'ambition's debt is paid'.
But it is also this same quality which, once his attention is
turned to the bloody reality of his action, impels him to
stagy ritual and political inaction, so that he may reconcile
the motive with the deed, or rather transform the deed
itself. He therefore commands the others to enact a scene
which both fulfils Calphurnia's dream, and also gives grue-
some reality to Brutus's own previous desire to sacrifice
Caesar as a dish fit for the gods:

> *Stoop, Romans, stoop,*
> *And let us bathe our hands in Caesar's blood*
> *Up to the elbows, and besmear our swords;*
> *Then walk we forth, even to the market-place,*
> *And waving our red weapons o'er our heads,*
> *Let's all cry, 'Peace, freedom, and liberty!'*
>   III.1.105–10

The conspirators' will to act appears to be paralysed as
they ironically comment on the play itself, in seeing their
deed as material for the theatres of the future:

CASSIUS   *How many ages hence*
  Shall this our lofty scene be acted over,
  In states unborn, and accents yet unknown!
BRUTUS
  How many times shall Caesar bleed in sport,
  That now on Pompey's basis lies along,
  No worthier than the dust!   III.1.111–16

Just as the initiative in the early part of the play lay with
the murderers of Caesar rather than with Caesar himself,
so now the initiative passes from the conspirators' own
hands. In order to make the point, Shakespeare begins to
develop the character of Antony who so far has been
merely 'a limb of Caesar's'. Cassius has galvanized the
still-bemused Brutus into some kind of action:

                    Ay, every man away.
    Brutus shall lead, and we will grace his heels
    With the most boldest and best hearts of Rome.
                                        III.1.119–21

Thereupon Antony's servant enters, quickly followed by
his master. What to Brutus was a bloody but necessary
sacrificial act is projected by Antony in a very different light.
For, in his words, Caesar's murder is seen as a hunt which
culminates in the death of a noble animal – 'a carcass fit
for hounds';

                  Here wast thou bayed, brave hart;
    Here didst thou fall; and here thy hunters stand,
    Signed in thy spoil, and crimsoned in thy lethe.
                                        III.1.204–6

And what Brutus saw as sacrificial blood becomes in his
mouth the badge of guilt with which the conspirators'
hands 'reek and smoke'. Using a subtle mixture of flattery

and hypocritical promise, Antony works upon Brutus to gain one concession – that he be allowed to speak at Caesar's funeral. Again there is a recapitulation of the tensions of the conspiracy which showed themselves on the night before the murder. Cassius, on the one hand, is full of shrewd misgivings about Antony's intentions and seeks to make specific the latter's vague promises of friendship:

> *Will you be pricked in number of our friends,*
> *Or shall we on, and not depend on you?*   III.1.216–17

And, knowing Antony better than we do at this point in the play, he offers material inducements:

> *Your voice shall be as strong as any man's*
> *In the disposing of new dignities.*   III.1.177–8

But again it is Brutus that prevails, and Antony is given permission to speak.

As Antony moves to a more central position on the stage, it is clear that his character partakes of a duality similar to those we have seen in Brutus, Cassius, and Caesar. On the one hand, there is present the genuine affection for Caesar the man, the admiration of what he was, and the loyalty to the memory of a dead friend, all of which come across in Antony's lines as he stands in the presence of Caesar's blood-stained enemies. There is, for example, no calculation, but rather total sincerity, in his words to Cassius which might well have damaged the cause he is about,

> *Pardon me, Caius Cassius;*
> *The enemies of Caesar shall say this;*
> *Then, in a friend, it is cold modesty.*   III.1.211–13

This affection is given fuller expression when he is left

alone with Caesar's corpse, as he drops into the easy
rhetoric which is one aspect of his character:

> *O, pardon me, thou bleeding piece of earth,*
> *That I am meek and gentle with these butchers.*
> *Thou art the ruins of the noblest man*
> *That ever livèd in the tide of times.*   III.1.254–7

But even as Antony displays this complete emotional
sincerity, the other side of his character, which we have
seen in action in his exchanges with the conspirators,
comes to the fore: namely, his skill in political manoeuvre.
From this point onwards, his deep-felt grief is to be sub-
sumed into his effort to bring about the destruction of
Brutus and his party, and make good his prophecy that

> *Caesar's spirit, ranging for revenge,*
> *With Ate by his side, come hot from hell,*
> *Shall in these confines with a monarch's voice*
> *Cry havoc and let slip the dogs of war,*
> *That this foul deed shall smell above the earth*
> *With carrion men, groaning for burial.* III.1.270–75

In order to achieve this, he combines ruthless determination with a coldly calculated employment of his gifts as an
orator to rouse the Roman mob to fury.

Antony's funeral oration is, of course, a masterly blend
of emotional appeal and false logic; and Shakespeare deliberately contrasts it with Brutus's carefully phrased and
politically skilful justification of his action. By using two
contrasting facts – Brutus's claim of the existence of
Caesar's ambition, and the fleshly reality of the body which
has suffered for it – Antony leads an initially hostile crowd
first to sympathy and then on to violence. If the 'noble'
Brutus has said Caesar was ambitious, it is 'grievously' that
'Caesar hath answered it'. The honour of Brutus is seen to

be denied ultimately by the coffin in which Caesar lies present on the stage; and the intentions of the conspiracy, by the rents their daggers made in Caesar's gown. These two aspects of the murder are used by Antony to build up to the moment of climax as he stands with Caesar's promised testament in his hands, and reveals, initially the torn mantle which Caesar wore first at his greatest victory, and then the body itself marred by traitors' hands. In the words of Antony, Caesar's carcass does indeed become the religious relic that Brutus would have it:

> *And they would go and kiss dead Caesar's wounds,*
> *And dip their napkins in his sacred blood,*
> *Yea, beg a hair of him for memory,*
> *And, dying, mention it within their wills,*
> *Bequeathing it as a rich legacy*
> *Unto their issue.*   III.2.133–8

As such, it is properly burnt in the holy places. However, this corpse is at the same time a remnant of Caesar's spirit, which Antony has seen as being also the spirit of discord; and Shakespeare gives us a brief but terrifying glimpse of the resulting riot in the death of the innocent poet, Cinna.

THE AFTERMATH

In the remaining acts of the play we see the murder's consequences, and the nature of the two parties in conflict. In the newly established triumvirate, the Machiavellian trait in Antony begins to dominate his character, and the would-be rulers of the Roman world, opposing Brutus and Cassius, are depicted as unscrupulous, ruthless, and cynical in the exercise of their present power. The Antony who viewed the murder of one man as the ultimate crime can now barter the life of his sister's son for that of Lepidus's brother. He can also slightingly dismiss one of his partners as 'unmeritable' and plot with Octavius to employ him as a scapegoat for their more culpable actions. With both his partners he can arrange to channel some part of Caesar's legacy into their own pockets.

The party opposing these men is no less divided, though for different reasons. Those qualities in Brutus and Cassius which in the earlier scenes made the conspiracy never more than a precariously balanced alliance are now seen in far more striking colours. The fundamental division between them, which previously had been suppressed by Brutus's confident idealism and Cassius's willingness to give way, is transformed into open and violent conflict. Brutus's confidence has hardened into a convinced belief in his own rightness on all topics; and Cassius tries in vain to make Brutus see the exigencies of their situation. The quarrel between them mirrors the inner quarrel that each man carries with him. For, as Brutus loved Caesar even as he struck him, so now, unless he is to admit the error of his decision, he must preserve his theory-based philosophy of life by keeping his actions and motives free from all the impurities of moral expediency. Thus while his military state demands immediate finance, it is Cassius who must supply him because, as he says,

> *I can raise no money by vile means;*
> *By heaven, I had rather coin my heart,*
> *And drop my blood for drachmas, than to wring*
> *From the hard hands of peasants their vile trash*
> *By any indirection.*   IV.3.71–5

Cassius himself is still plagued by his need for close personal relationship, and is painfully conscious of the ideals that Brutus represents. But he is also irritated by the form these ideals take in regard to himself, and the impediment they constitute to the success of their cause in practical matters. On the one hand, he feels strongly that he is

> Hated by one he loves; braved by his brother;
> Checked like a bondman; all his faults observed,
> Set in a notebook, learned, and conned by rote,
> To cast into my teeth. O, I could weep
> My spirit from mine eyes!   IV.3.95–9

On the other hand, he realizes with agonized clarity that at such a time, despite the large issues of the ides of March, and the noble sentiments concerning, say, justice, or vile but necessary 'rascal counters',

> it is not meet
> That every nice offence should bear his comment. IV.3.7–8

In spite of the amity restored at the end of the quarrel scene, both Brutus and Cassius carry their divisions into the final battle. Brutus, with the knowledge that Caesar's spirit has not been stilled either physically or metaphorically, begins to realize that what he had taken to be a purely political act has become far more significant for him as a useless violation of personal trust. He enters the battle at Philippi with an unconscious feeling of fate hanging over him:

> There is a tide in the affairs of men,
> Which, taken at the flood, leads on to fortune;
> Omitted, all the voyage of their life
> Is bound in shallows and in miseries.   IV.3.216–19

Nevertheless, it is his singleminded, though tactically ill-judged, fervour that enables him both to defeat Octavius's wing of the army, and to neglect Cassius's failure against Antony.

As each man dies, he characteristically reacts to the 'work the ides of March begun'. In Cassius's case, the vow to die is the result of a combination of literal short-sightedness and what he views as a betrayal of friendship and his recognition of yet another error by Brutus. But the form his death takes harks back to the material motives which lay behind his deed in killing Caesar: he offers Caesar merely a life for a life, with the same sword:

> Caesar, thou art revenged,
> Even with the sword that killed thee.   V.3.45–6

For Brutus, the end is different; surrounded by loyal and loving friends, he can reassert his belief in the rightness of his part in the conspiracy as he saw it:

> My heart doth joy that yet in all my life
> I found no man but he was true to me.
> I shall have glory by this losing day
> More than Octavius and Mark Antony
> By this vile conquest shall attain unto.   V.5.34–8

And at the moment of death he reverts to the strange inner contradiction which his decision to kill his friend represented:

> Caesar, now be still;
> I killed not thee with half so good a will.   V.5.50–51

For the winning triumvirate, there is the future parting of the spoils and the hinted promise of future strife between Antony, who can give eloquent appreciation of Brutus's qualities, and the silent Octavius, who has become 'another Caesar' crossing his partner simply because he 'will do so'.

THE POETRY AND THE PLAY

Certainly the most immediately striking feature of the play is the clash between the personalities of the great central figures as they wrestle with huge national issues and their own inner lives. Shakespeare, however, wrote poetic drama, and it is by poetic as well as dramatic means that the many other themes are incorporated into the whole, and by which the politico-personal tension is set in a far wider context. It is true that Shakespeare created for this play a largely unmetaphorical and unlyrical style, which derives its power from strong sentence structure and simple rhythms rather than from any associative richness; clarity and dignity are its qualities, not complexity and allusiveness, which are more usual in Shakespeare. Nevertheless, the poetry of the play is threaded through with major and minor patterns of imagery, which appear in the form in which ideas are expressed, or in simile and metaphor, or in described incident; and which are given body in the physical actions which take place on the stage. There have been several full-length analyses of these 'chains of imagery'; but some of those observed may be mentioned briefly to illustrate the way in which they widen the play's scope.

Most of these images attach themselves to the basic political and personal conflicts in the play, knitting them together and providing each with additional perspectives. For example, the image of blood is invested with multiple associations. For Antony, it is the wantonly-spilt blood of the noblest man in the tide of times; as such it is at once the sign of guilt smeared on the conspirators' arms 'up to the elbows', and the tincture which will make sacred handkerchiefs dipped in it. To Brutus, it is the blood which is let regrettably in a necessary sacrifice to save the Roman body politic which has grown rank. In many speeches it is linked with metallic images of hacking and cutting, or with those of value; and these in turn are connected with animal imagery of stag-hunting and bleeding carcasses, all of which are given additional power by the presence of

Caesar's mutilated body which lies in the audience's view during the two climax-scenes of the play. In a similar way, there is a close connexion between the concepts of friendship and love, and the images of fire and affection. These can be hideously destructive in combination, as they are when Portia, for the love of a Brutus exiled, swallows fire; or when the mob take from Caesar's funeral pyre brands to fire the conspirators' houses. But these things can also be the signals of human sympathy, as when Cassius 'cannot drink too much of Brutus' love', or when Antony's eyes are 'red as fire with weeping'. These and the other image patterns the play contains, such as those connected with storm and disorder, acting and the stage, the physical aspects of the city, the human body, sleep, and the spiritual world, are linked at every point with one another and with the more obvious issues, and greatly enrich the imaginative vision of the whole.

Most critics of the play have been in agreement about its various poetic and dramatic excellences; but they have disagreed frequently in trying to define what *kind* of play it is. On the one hand, it has been seen as the tragedy of Brutus; and there are, in its pattern, sufficient similarities to the great tragedies which were to follow to support this view. For in Brutus, as we have seen, we are presented with the victim of an inner conflict, who is worked upon by outside forces, and torn between two basic impulses in his own nature: the rival claims of personal relationships and of the public good. He is a man forced to make a moral choice which, once taken, is irrevocable, and which has its implications both for the macrocosm and the microcosm. As the action progresses there is traced the hideous interim between the 'first motion' and 'the acting of a dreadful thing', and then its consequences, and finally the tragic disillusionment.

To other critics, however, Brutus is not central to the play as Hamlet or Macbeth are to theirs, and some have pointed out that, although he has many of the traits which suggest the lines along which a tragic hero may be constructed, he is in fact a character of another sort of play – namely, a history play. These writers see Shakespeare focusing his attention on the historic and political significances of the conspiracy itself, and able to do so with a calm and dispassionate scrutiny because he was free of the patriotic overtones which the material of the English history plays had forced upon him.

Still other scholars have taken another approach, arguing that, while the moral issue of the play is indeed fought out in Brutus, Shakespeare shaped his material and characters – particularly Caesar – with deliberate ambiguity, in order to present a pair of unanswered problems as to the nature of the true Caesar, and as to the justifiability of the conspiracy against him.

Yet it is not strictly necessary either, because of its similarities to *Macbeth* or *Hamlet*, to force the play into the mould of that kind of tragedy; or to class it with *Measure for Measure* because of the type of problems it raises; or to make it an 'abstract' history play because its themes draw it close to *Henry VI* or *Richard II*. The play both in the theatre and in the classroom has proved its ability to stand on its own. It raises complex questions, like every great work of art, and answers some of them in its own complex terms; that it also presents problems to which there are no final solutions, either in the play or outside of it, is a measure of its success, not its failure.

FURTHER READING

T. S. Dorsch's Arden edition of the play (1955), A. R. Humphreys' Oxford edition (1984) and Marvin Spevack's New Cambridge edition (1988) provide the reader with a choice of carefully edited texts. As the editors are dealing with what is probably the best printed of Shakespeare's plays, and one of those found only in the 1623 Folio, there are no really difficult or controversial matters arising from the transmission of the text – which doesn't mean to say, as Spevack points out, that there are no textual problems at all. Still, their relative absence permits the plays' editors to join their fellow readers in the sometimes frustrating business of making sense of what is widely recognized as one of Shakespeare's most enigmatic plays. As Humphreys notes: 'It is the first of Shakespeare's tragedies in which moral bewilderments become fundamentally important.' Characters (and readers) are morally bewildered, Humphreys believes, because the play is in the 'Hegelian tragic category where good struggles not with evil but with incompatible good'. So, despite the fact that, as Dorsch points out, the play's main speeches are characterized by 'clarity, directness and simplicity', the 'manliness' of the play's style is in the service of a delicacy and complexity of interpretation. Shades of *Coriolanus*.

The play's central characters, Brutus and Caesar, carry the main burden of interpretative delicacy. How are we to understand them? We can only do so, as many critics have argued, by coming to terms first of all with Shakespeare's sophisticated presentation of the politics of Republican Rome. We need to see the main characters against their schismatic background. Jan H. Blits's collection of essays, *The End of the*

43

Ancient Republic: Essays on 'Julius Caesar' (1982), examines the depths of the play's ambiguity against this background; Blits is one of many who find Caesar, in particular, difficult to fathom. So does Norman Rabkin in his highly influential book *Shakespeare and the Problem of Meaning* (1981): *Julius Caesar* is a play, he says, in which Shakespeare presents 'one of the defining moments in world history in such a way that his audience cannot determine whether the protagonist is the best or worst of men'. This enigmatic presentation of Caesar's character and motives makes the play a central one in Ernest Schanzer's *The Problem Plays of Shakespeare* (1963). And Robert Miola's *Shakespeare's Rome* (1983) insists upon 'the complexity and ambivalence of Caesar's story'. Harold Bloom's collection of essays in the Major Literary Characters Series (1994) discusses treatments of Julius Caesar by Shakespeare, Shaw, Lucan and Brecht. Of Shakespeare's Caesar, Bloom writes: 'There is an extraordinary blend of uncanniness and vainglory in Shakespeare's Caesar but the uncanniness or sublimity seems to me the stronger element.' As Derek Traversi points out in *Shakespeare: the Roman Plays* (1963), interpretation is necessarily clouded by the way the play presents the 'contrast between what men propose, and what, as political beings, they in fact achieve'. J. L. Simmons, in *Shakespeare's Pagan World: The Roman Tragedies* (1973), connects the enigmatic presentation of Caesar with the ambivalences of Shakespeare's Histories. Charles Wells's *The Wide Arch: Roman Values in Shakespeare* (1992) talks of *Julius Caesar* almost entirely in terms of its exploitation of ambiguity.

At least Rabkin, Miola and others seem to be certain as to just who the play's protagonist is. Others are by no means so sure. Some plump for Brutus, others for Caesar, while Waldo F. McNeir denies the claim of both candidates in his *Shakespeare's 'Julius Caesar': A Tragedy without a Hero* (1970). For Spevack in the New Cambridge edition the focus of the play is so clearly on Brutus that he cannot understand what all the fuss is about. T. S. Dorsch, in his Arden edition, also believes Brutus to be the dramatic hero, though, unlike Plutarch's Brutus, he is 'with all his estimable qualities, pompous, opinionated and self-righteous' (whereas Caesar grows in stature as the play proceeds). This is also Blits's view: 'Deprecating political results, Brutus ultimately disdains humanity.' Alexander Leggatt's *Shakespeare's Political Drama: The History Plays and the Roman Plays* (1988) talks about Brutus's detachment from reality, his inability to see the tyrannical impulses already manifested in Caesar. This is because 'in this Roman world of ex-schoolboys the strongest emotional attachments are between men' – or between men and boys: only with Lucius, the servant-boy, can Brutus truly relax.

Hence main characters and play are something of a puzzle, and no less entertaining for being so. For this we can thank Shakespeare's imaginative re-ordering and sophisticating of history. Vivian Thomas's *Shakespeare's Roman Worlds* (1989) emphasizes the enterprising difference between Shakespeare's invention and his sources, while, in something of a diatribe on source hunters, Spevack asserts that 'Shakespeare's dependence on Plutarch is, it should be clear, the measure of his independence.' Such is Shakespeare's independence, Blits argues, that it's possible to claim that Caesar's death is the end, not the salvation, of Republican Rome. Among other good things, Blits's collection of essays explores Shakespeare's felicitous jugglings with notions of manliness. Ironically enough, he says: 'The specific character of manly virtues is indicated by Portia, who gashes herself in the thigh to prove that she's strong enough to keep Brutus' secret plans in confidence.'

It's arguable that a play as designedly indeterminate as *Julius Caesar* requires a strong selection of good introductory material. This can be found in Allan Bloom's *Shakespeare's Politics* (1964), Adrien Bonjour's *The Structure of 'Julius Caesar'* (1958), Nicholas Brooke's *Shakespeare's Early Tragedies* (1968), L. F. Dean's Twentieth Century Interpretations (1968), Julian Markels's *Shakespeare's 'Julius Caesar'* (1961) (the text of the play and a collection of essays), and Mungo MacCallum's *Shakespeare's Roman Plays and their Background* (1967). *Shakespeare Survey* 10 (1957) is devoted to the Roman plays. Brents Stirling's *The Populace in Shakespeare* (1947) discusses this aspect of the play in the context of the *Second Part of Henry VI* and *Coriolanus*. Maurice Charney's *Shakespeare's Roman Plays: The Function of Imagery in the Drama* (1963) studies *Julius Caesar*, *Antony and Cleopatra* and *Coriolanus* as 'poetry of the theater', and John Ripley's *'Julius Caesar' on Stage in England and America, 1599–1973* (1980) traces the plays' stage history as 'a tale of unrealized potential'.

Michael Taylor, 1996

JULIUS CAESAR

THE CHARACTERS IN THE PLAY

JULIUS CAESAR
CALPHURNIA, his wife

MARCUS BRUTUS
CAIUS CASSIUS
CASCA
TREBONIUS
DECIUS BRUTUS }conspirators against Caesar
METELLUS CIMBER
CINNA
CAIUS LIGARIUS

OCTAVIUS CAESAR
MARK ANTONY }triumvirs after Caesar's death
LEPIDUS

CICERO
PUBLIUS }Senators
POPILIUS LENA

FLAVIUS }Tribunes of the People
MARULLUS

LUCILIUS
MESSALA
YOUNG CATO
VOLUMNIUS
TITINIUS }followers of Brutus and Cassius
VARRO
CLITUS
CLAUDIUS
DARDANIUS

THE CHARACTERS IN THE PLAY

PORTIA, Marcus Brutus's wife
ARTEMIDORUS
CINNA, a poet
PINDARUS, a servant of Cassius
LUCIUS }
STRATO } servants of Brutus

A Soothsayer
A Poet
A Cobbler
A Carpenter
A Servant of Caesar
A Servant of Antony
A Servant of Octavius
The Ghost of Caesar
Senators
Soldiers, Plebeians, Attendants and others

Enter Flavius, Marullus, and certain commoners over 1.1
the stage

FLAVIUS

Hence! home, you idle creatures, get you home:
Is this a holiday? What, know you not,
Being mechanical, you ought not walk
Upon a labouring day without the sign
Of your profession? Speak, what trade art thou?

CARPENTER Why, sir, a carpenter.

MARULLUS

Where is thy leather apron, and thy rule?
What dost thou with thy best apparel on?
You, sir, what trade are you?

COBBLER Truly, sir, in respect of a fine workman, I   10
am but, as you would say, a cobbler.

MARULLUS But what trade art thou? Answer me directly.

COBBLER A trade, sir, that I hope I may use with a safe
conscience; which is, indeed, sir, a mender of bad soles.

FLAVIUS

What trade, thou knave? Thou naughty knave, what
trade?

COBBLER Nay, I beseech you, sir, be not out with me:
yet if you be out, sir, I can mend you.

MARULLUS

What meanest thou by that? Mend me, thou saucy
fellow?

COBBLER Why, sir, cobble you.

FLAVIUS Thou art a cobbler, art thou?

COBBLER Truly, sir, all that I live by is with the awl: I
meddle with no tradesman's matters, nor women's matters; but withal I am, indeed, sir, a surgeon to old shoes:
when they are in great danger, I recover them. As proper
men as ever trod upon neat's leather have gone upon
my handiwork.

FLAVIUS
But wherefore art not in thy shop today?
Why dost thou lead these men about the streets?

COBBLER Truly, sir, to wear out their shoes to get myself
30 into more work. But indeed, sir, we make holiday to see
Caesar, and to rejoice in his triumph.

MARULLUS
Wherefore rejoice? What conquest brings he home?
What tributaries follow him to Rome,
To grace in captive bonds his chariot wheels?
You blocks, you stones, you worse than senseless things!
O you hard hearts, you cruel men of Rome,
Knew you not Pompey? Many a time and oft
Have you climbed up to walls and battlements,
To towers and windows, yea, to chimney-tops,
40 Your infants in your arms, and there have sat
The livelong day, with patient expectation,
To see great Pompey pass the streets of Rome:
And when you saw his chariot but appear,
Have you not made an universal shout,
That Tiber trembled underneath her banks
To hear the replication of your sounds
Made in her concave shores?
And do you now put on your best attire?
And do you now cull out a holiday?
50 And do you now strew flowers in his way,
That comes in triumph over Pompey's blood?
Be gone!

Run to your houses, fall upon your knees,
Pray to the gods to intermit the plague
That needs must light on this ingratitude.

FLAVIUS

Go, go, good countrymen, and for this fault
Assemble all the poor men of your sort;
Draw them to Tiber banks, and weep your tears
Into the channel, till the lowest stream
Do kiss the most exalted shores of all.   60

Exeunt all the commoners

See where their basest mettle be not moved:
They vanish tongue-tied in their guiltiness.
Go you down that way towards the Capitol;
This way will I. Disrobe the images,
If you do find them decked with ceremonies.

MARULLUS May we do so?
You know it is the feast of Lupercal.

FLAVIUS

It is no matter; let no images
Be hung with Caesar's trophies. I'll about,
And drive away the vulgar from the streets;   70
So do you too, where you perceive them thick.
These growing feathers plucked from Caesar's wing
Will make him fly an ordinary pitch,
Who else would soar above the view of men,
And keep us all in servile fearfulness.   *Exeunt*

Enter Caesar; Antony, stripped for the course; Cal- I.2
phurnia, Portia, Decius, Cicero, Brutus, Cassius,
Casca, a Soothsayer, and a great crowd; after them
Marullus and Flavius.

CAESAR

Calphurnia.

53

CASCA   Peace, ho! Caesar speaks.

CAESAR   Calphurnia.

CALPHURNIA Here, my lord.

CAESAR

Stand you directly in Antonius' way
When he doth run his course. Antonius.

ANTONY Caesar, my lord?

CAESAR

Forget not, in your speed, Antonius,
To touch Calphurnia; for our elders say,
The barren, touchèd in this holy chase,
Shake off their sterile curse.

ANTONY   I shall remember:

10 When Caesar says, 'Do this', it is performed.

CAESAR

Set on, and leave no ceremony out.

SOOTHSAYER Caesar!

CAESAR Ha! Who calls?

CASCA

Bid every noise be still; peace yet again!

CAESAR

Who is it in the press that calls on me?
I hear a tongue shriller than all the music
Cry 'Caesar!' Speak. Caesar is turned to hear.

SOOTHSAYER

Beware the ides of March.

CAESAR   What man is that?

BRUTUS

A soothsayer bids you beware the ides of March.

CAESAR

20 Set him before me; let me see his face.

CASSIUS

Fellow, come from the throng; look upon Caesar.

54

CAESAR

What sayst thou to me now? Speak once again.

SOOTHSAYER Beware the ides of March.

CAESAR

He is a dreamer. Let us leave him. Pass.

Sennet. Exeunt

Brutus and Cassius remain

CASSIUS

Will you go see the order of the course?

BRUTUS Not I.

CASSIUS I pray you, do.

BRUTUS

I am not gamesome: I do lack some part
Of that quick spirit that is in Antony.
Let me not hinder, Cassius, your desires;
I'll leave you.

CASSIUS

Brutus, I do observe you now of late:
I have not from your eyes that gentleness
And show of love as I was wont to have.
You bear too stubborn and too strange a hand
Over your friend that loves you.

BRUTUS   Cassius,
Be not deceived: if I have veiled my look,
I turn the trouble of my countenance
Merely upon myself. Vexèd I am
Of late with passions of some difference,
Conceptions only proper to myself,
Which give some soil, perhaps, to my behaviours;
But let not therefore my good friends be grieved –
Among which number, Cassius, be you one –
Nor construe any further my neglect,
Than that poor Brutus, with himself at war,
Forgets the shows of love to other men.

55

CASSIUS

    Then, Brutus, I have much mistook your passion,
    By means whereof this breast of mine hath buried
50   Thoughts of great value, worthy cogitations.
    Tell me, good Brutus, can you see your face?

BRUTUS

    No, Cassius; for the eye sees not itself
    But by reflection, by some other things.

CASSIUS 'Tis just;

    And it is very much lamented, Brutus,
    That you have no such mirrors as will turn
    Your hidden worthiness into your eye,
    That you might see your shadow. I have heard,
    Where many of the best respect in Rome,
60   Except immortal Caesar, speaking of Brutus,
    And groaning underneath this age's yoke,
    Have wished that noble Brutus had his eyes.

BRUTUS

    Into what dangers would you lead me, Cassius,
    That you would have me seek into myself
    For that which is not in me?

CASSIUS

    Therefore, good Brutus, be prepared to hear;
    And since you know you cannot see yourself
    So well as by reflection, I, your glass,
    Will modestly discover to yourself
70   That of yourself which you yet know not of.
    And be not jealous on me, gentle Brutus:
    Were I a common laughter, or did use
    To stale with ordinary oaths my love
    To every new protester; if you know
    That I do fawn on men and hug them hard,
    And after scandal them; or if you know
    That I profess myself in banqueting

To all the rout, then hold me dangerous.
   Flourish and shout

BRUTUS

What means this shouting? I do fear the people
Choose Caesar for their king.

CASSIUS   Ay, do you fear it?   80
Then must I think you would not have it so.

BRUTUS

I would not, Cassius; yet I love him well.
But wherefore do you hold me here so long?
What is it that you would impart to me?
If it be aught toward the general good,
Set honour in one eye, and death i'th'other,
And I will look on both indifferently;
For let the gods so speed me as I love
The name of honour more than I fear death.

CASSIUS

I know that virtue to be in you, Brutus,   90
As well as I do know your outward favour.
Well, honour is the subject of my story.
I cannot tell what you and other men
Think of this life; but for my single self,
I had as lief not be as live to be
In awe of such a thing as I myself.
I was born free as Caesar, so were you;
We both have fed as well, and we can both
Endure the winter's cold as well as he.
For once, upon a raw and gusty day,   100
The troubled Tiber chafing with her shores,
Caesar said to me, 'Dar'st thou, Cassius, now
Leap in with me into this angry flood,
And swim to yonder point?' Upon the word,
Accoutrèd as I was, I plungèd in
And bade him follow; so indeed he did.

The torrent roared, and we did buffet it
With lusty sinews, throwing it aside
And stemming it with hearts of controversy.
110 But ere we could arrive the point proposed,
Caesar cried, 'Help me, Cassius, or I sink!'
I, as Aeneas, our great ancestor,
Did from the flames of Troy upon his shoulder
The old Anchises bear, so from the waves of Tiber
Did I the tired Caesar. And this man
Is now become a god, and Cassius is
A wretched creature, and must bend his body
If Caesar carelessly but nod on him.
He had a fever when he was in Spain,
120 And when the fit was on him, I did mark
How he did shake; 'tis true, this god did shake;
His coward lips did from their colour fly,
And that same eye whose bend doth awe the world
Did lose his lustre; I did hear him groan;
Ay, and that tongue of his, that bade the Romans
Mark him and write his speeches in their books,
'Alas!' it cried, 'Give me some drink, Titinius',
As a sick girl. Ye gods, it doth amaze me
A man of such a feeble temper should
130 So get the start of the majestic world,
And bear the palm alone.
  Shout. Flourish
BRUTUS   Another general shout?
I do believe that these applauses are
For some new honours that are heaped on Caesar.
CASSIUS
Why, man, he doth bestride the narrow world
Like a Colossus, and we petty men
Walk under his huge legs, and peep about
To find ourselves dishonourable graves.

Men at some time are masters of their fates;
The fault, dear Brutus, is not in our stars,
But in ourselves, that we are underlings. 140
Brutus and Caesar. What should be in that 'Caesar'?
Why should that name be sounded more than yours?
Write them together, yours is as fair a name;
Sound them, it doth become the mouth as well;
Weigh them, it is as heavy; conjure with 'em,
'Brutus' will start a spirit as soon as 'Caesar'.
Now in the names of all the gods at once,
Upon what meat doth this our Caesar feed,
That he is grown so great? Age, thou art shamed!
Rome, thou hast lost the breed of noble bloods! 150
When went there by an age, since the great flood,
But it was famed with more than with one man?
When could they say, till now, that talked of Rome,
That her wide walls encompassed but one man?
Now is it Rome indeed, and room enough,
When there is in it but one only man.
O, you and I have heard our fathers say,
There was a Brutus once that would have brooked
Th'eternal devil to keep his state in Rome
As easily as a king. 160

BRUTUS
That you do love me, I am nothing jealous;
What you would work me to, I have some aim:
How I have thought of this, and of these times,
I shall recount hereafter. For this present,
I would not – so with love I might entreat you –
Be any further moved. What you have said
I will consider; what you have to say
I will with patience hear, and find a time
Both meet to hear and answer such high things.
Till then, my noble friend, chew upon this: 170

59

Brutus had rather be a villager
Than to repute himself a son of Rome
Under these hard conditions as this time
Is like to lay upon us.

CASSIUS   I am glad
That my weak words have struck but thus much show
Of fire from Brutus.

Enter Caesar and his train

BRUTUS

The games are done and Caesar is returning.

CASSIUS

As they pass by, pluck Casca by the sleeve,
And he will, after his sour fashion, tell you
180 What hath proceeded worthy note today.

BRUTUS

I will do so. But look you, Cassius,
The angry spot doth glow on Caesar's brow,
And all the rest look like a chidden train:
Calphurnia's cheek is pale, and Cicero
Looks with such ferret and such fiery eyes
As we have seen him in the Capitol
Being crossed in conference by some senators.

CASSIUS

Casca will tell us what the matter is.

CAESAR Antonius.

190 ANTONY Caesar?

CAESAR

Let me have men about me that are fat,
Sleek-headed men, and such as sleep a-nights.
Yond Cassius has a lean and hungry look;
He thinks too much: such men are dangerous.

ANTONY

Fear him not, Caesar; he's not dangerous;
He is a noble Roman, and well given.

CAESAR

Would he were fatter! But I fear him not;
Yet if my name were liable to fear,
I do not know the man I should avoid
So soon as that spare Cassius. He reads much,   200
He is a great observer, and he looks
Quite through the deeds of men. He loves no plays,
As thou dost, Antony; he hears no music;
Seldom he smiles, and smiles in such a sort
As if he mocked himself, and scorned his spirit
That could be moved to smile at anything.
Such men as he be never at heart's ease
Whiles they behold a greater than themselves,
And therefore are they very dangerous.
I rather tell thee what is to be feared   210
Than what I fear; for always I am Caesar.
Come on my right hand, for this ear is deaf,
And tell me truly what thou think'st of him.

Sennet. Exeunt Caesar and his train

CASCA

You pulled me by the cloak; would you speak with me?

BRUTUS

Ay, Casca, tell us what hath chanced today
That Caesar looks so sad.

CASCA Why, you were with him, were you not?

BRUTUS

I should not then ask Casca what had chanced.

CASCA Why, there was a crown offered him; and, being
offered him, he put it by with the back of his hand, thus;   220
and then the people fell a-shouting.

BRUTUS What was the second noise for?

CASCA Why, for that too.

CASSIUS They shouted thrice: what was the last cry for?

CASCA Why, for that too.

BRUTUS Was the crown offered him thrice?

CASCA Ay, marry, was't, and he put it by thrice, every time gentler than other; and at every putting-by mine honest neighbours shouted.

230 CASSIUS Who offered him the crown?

CASCA Why, Antony.

BRUTUS Tell us the manner of it, gentle Casca.

CASCA I can as well be hanged as tell the manner of it; it was mere foolery; I did not mark it. I saw Mark Antony offer him a crown; yet 'twas not a crown neither, 'twas one of these coronets; and, as I told you, he put it by once; but for all that, to my thinking, he would fain have had it. Then he offered it to him again; then he put it by again; but to my thinking, he was very loath to lay his 240 fingers off it. And then he offered it the third time; he put it the third time by; and still as he refused it, the rabblement hooted, and clapped their chopped hands, and threw up their sweaty night-caps, and uttered such a deal of stinking breath because Caesar refused the crown, that it had, almost, choked Caesar; for he swooned, and fell down at it. And for mine own part, I durst not laugh, for fear of opening my lips and receiving the bad air.

CASSIUS

But soft, I pray you; what, did Caesar swoon?

250 CASCA He fell down in the market-place, and foamed at mouth, and was speechless.

BRUTUS 'Tis very like; he hath the falling sickness.

CASSIUS

No, Caesar hath it not; but you, and I,
And honest Casca, we have the falling sickness.

CASCA I know not what you mean by that, but I am sure Caesar fell down. If the tag-rag people did not clap him and hiss him, according as he pleased and displeased

them, as they use to do the players in the theatre, I am
no true man.

BRUTUS

What said he when he came unto himself? 260

CASCA Marry, before he fell down, when he perceived the
common herd was glad he refused the crown, he
plucked me ope his doublet, and offered them his throat
to cut. An I had been a man of any occupation, if I
would not have taken him at a word, I would I might go
to hell among the rogues. And so he fell. When he came
to himself again, he said, if he had done or said anything
amiss, he desired their worships to think it was his infirmity. Three or four wenches, where I stood, cried,
'Alas, good soul!' and forgave him with all their hearts; 270
but there's no heed to be taken of them; if Caesar had
stabbed their mothers, they would have done no less.

BRUTUS

And after that, he came thus sad away?

CASCA Ay.

CASSIUS Did Cicero say anything?

CASCA Ay, he spoke Greek.

CASSIUS To what effect?

CASCA Nay, an I tell you that, I'll ne'er look you i'th'face
again. But those that understood him smiled at one another, and shook their heads; but for mine own part, it 280
was Greek to me. I could tell you more news too:
Marullus and Flavius, for pulling scarfs off Caesar's
images, are put to silence. Fare you well. There was more
foolery yet, if I could remember it.

CASSIUS Will you sup with me tonight, Casca?

CASCA No, I am promised forth.

CASSIUS Will you dine with me tomorrow?

CASCA Ay, if I be alive, and your mind hold, and your
dinner worth the eating.

290 CASSIUS Good; I will expect you.

CASCA Do so. Farewell, both. *Exit*

BRUTUS

What a blunt fellow is this grown to be!
He was quick mettle when he went to school.

CASSIUS

So is he now in execution
Of any bold or noble enterprise,
However he puts on this tardy form.
This rudeness is a sauce to his good wit,
Which gives men stomach to disgest his words
With better appetite.

BRUTUS

300 And so it is. For this time I will leave you.
Tomorrow, if you please to speak with me,
I will come home to you; or if you will,
Come home to me, and I will wait for you.

CASSIUS

I will do so: till then, think of the world. *Exit Brutus*
Well, Brutus, thou art noble; yet I see
Thy honourable mettle may be wrought
From that it is disposed: therefore it is meet
That noble minds keep ever with their likes;
For who so firm that cannot be seduced?

310 Caesar doth bear me hard, but he loves Brutus.
If I were Brutus now, and he were Cassius,
He should not humour me. I will this night,
In several hands, in at his windows throw,
As if they came from several citizens,
Writings, all tending to the great opinion
That Rome holds of his name; wherein obscurely
Caesar's ambition shall be glancèd at.
And after this, let Caesar seat him sure,
For we will shake him, or worse days endure. *Exit*

Enter Casca and Cicero, meeting

CICERO

Good even, Casca: brought you Caesar home?
Why are you breathless? and why stare you so?

CASCA

Are not you moved, when all the sway of earth
Shakes like a thing unfirm? O Cicero,
I have seen tempests, when the scolding winds
Have rived the knotty oaks, and I have seen
Th'ambitious ocean swell and rage and foam,
To be exalted with the threatening clouds;
But never till tonight, never till now,
Did I go through a tempest dropping fire.   10
Either there is a civil strife in heaven,
Or else the world, too saucy with the gods,
Incenses them to send destruction.

CICERO

Why, saw you anything more wonderful?

CASCA

A common slave – you know him well by sight –
Held up his left hand, which did flame and burn
Like twenty torches joined; and yet his hand,
Not sensible of fire, remained unscorched.
Besides – I ha'not since put up my sword –
Against the Capitol I met a lion,   20
Who glazed upon me, and went surly by,
Without annoying me. And there were drawn
Upon a heap a hundred ghastly women,
Transformèd with their fear, who swore they saw
Men, all in fire, walk up and down the streets.
And yesterday the bird of night did sit,
Even at noon-day, upon the market-place,
Hooting and shrieking. When these prodigies

Do so conjointly meet, let not men say,
30 'These are their reasons, they are natural';
For I believe, they are portentous things
Unto the climate that they point upon.

CICERO

Indeed, it is a strange-disposèd time:
But men may construe things after their fashion,
Clean from the purpose of the things themselves.
Comes Caesar to the Capitol tomorrow?

CASCA

He doth; for he did bid Antonius
Send word to you he would be there tomorrow.

CICERO

Good night then, Casca: this disturbèd sky
40 Is not to walk in.

CASCA   Farewell, Cicero.   *Exit Cicero*
            Enter Cassius

CASSIUS

Who's there?

CASCA   A Roman.

CASSIUS   Casca, by your voice.

CASCA

Your ear is good. Cassius, what night is this!

CASSIUS

A very pleasing night to honest men.

CASCA

Who ever knew the heavens menace so?

CASSIUS

Those that have known the earth so full of faults.
For my part, I have walked about the streets,
Submitting me unto the perilous night,
And, thus unbracèd, Casca, as you see,
Have bared my bosom to the thunder-stone;
50 And when the cross blue lightning seemed to open

66

The breast of heaven, I did present myself
Even in the aim and very flash of it.

CASCA

But wherefore did you so much tempt the heavens?
It is the part of men to fear and tremble
When the most mighty gods by tokens send
Such dreadful heralds to astonish us.

CASSIUS

You are dull, Casca, and those sparks of life
That should be in a Roman you do want,
Or else you use not. You look pale, and gaze,
And put on fear, and cast yourself in wonder,   60
To see the strange impatience of the heavens;
But if you would consider the true cause
Why all these fires, why all these gliding ghosts,
Why birds and beasts from quality and kind,
Why old men, fools, and children calculate,
Why all these things change from their ordinance,
Their natures, and pre-formèd faculties,
To monstrous quality, why, you shall find
That heaven hath infused them with these spirits
To make them instruments of fear and warning   70
Unto some monstrous state.
Now could I, Casca, name to thee a man
Most like this dreadful night,
That thunders, lightens, opens graves, and roars
As doth the lion in the Capitol;
A man no mightier than thyself, or me,
In personal action, yet prodigious grown,
And fearful, as these strange eruptions are.

CASCA

'Tis Caesar that you mean; is it not, Cassius?

CASSIUS

Let it be who it is: for Romans now   80

67

Have thews and limbs like to their ancestors;
But woe the while! our fathers' minds are dead,
And we are governed with our mothers' spirits:
Our yoke and sufferance show us womanish.

CASCA

Indeed, they say the senators tomorrow
Mean to establish Caesar as a king;
And he shall wear his crown by sea and land,
In every place save here in Italy.

CASSIUS

I know where I will wear this dagger then:
90 Cassius from bondage will deliver Cassius.
Therein, ye gods, you make the weak most strong;
Therein, ye gods, you tyrants do defeat.
Nor stony tower, nor walls of beaten brass,
Nor airless dungeon, nor strong links of iron,
Can be retentive to the strength of spirit;
But life, being weary of these worldly bars,
Never lacks power to dismiss itself.
If I know this, know all the world besides,
That part of tyranny that I do bear
100 I can shake off at pleasure.

Thunder still

CASCA   So can I;
So every bondman in his own hand bears
The power to cancel his captivity.

CASSIUS

And why should Caesar be a tyrant then?
Poor man! I know he would not be a wolf,
But that he sees the Romans are but sheep.
He were no lion, were not Romans hinds.
Those that with haste will make a mighty fire
Begin it with weak straws. What trash is Rome,
What rubbish, and what offal, when it serves

68

For the base matter to illuminate   110
So vile a thing as Caesar! But, O grief,
Where hast thou led me? I perhaps speak this
Before a willing bondman; then I know
My answer must be made. But I am armed,
And dangers are to me indifferent.

CASCA

You speak to Casca, and to such a man
That is no fleering tell-tale. Hold, my hand;
Be factious for redress of all these griefs,
And I will set this foot of mine as far
As who goes farthest.

CASSIUS   There's a bargain made.   120
Now know you, Casca, I have moved already
Some certain of the noblest-minded Romans
To undergo with me an enterprise
Of honourable-dangerous consequence;
And I do know, by this they stay for me
In Pompey's Porch: for now, this fearful night,
There is no stir or walking in the streets;
And the complexion of the element
In favour's like the work we have in hand,
Most bloody, fiery, and most terrible.   130

Enter Cinna

CASCA

Stand close awhile, for here comes one in haste.

CASSIUS

'Tis Cinna; I do know him by his gait;
He is a friend. Cinna, where haste you so?

CINNA

To find out you. Who's that? Metellus Cimber?

CASSIUS

No, it is Casca, one incorporate
To our attempts. Am I not stayed for, Cinna?

CINNA

I am glad on't. What a fearful night is this!
There's two or three of us have seen strange sights.

CASSIUS

Am I not stayed for? Tell me.

CINNA   Yes, you are.

140 O Cassius, if you could
But win the noble Brutus to our party –

CASSIUS

Be you content. Good Cinna, take this paper,
And look you lay it in the praetor's chair,
Where Brutus may but find it; and throw this
In at his window; set this up with wax
Upon old Brutus' statue. All this done,
Repair to Pompey's Porch, where you shall find us.
Is Decius Brutus and Trebonius there?

CINNA

All but Metellus Cimber; and he's gone
150 To seek you at your house. Well, I will hie,
And so bestow these papers as you bade me.

CASSIUS

That done, repair to Pompey's Theatre.   *Exit Cinna*
Come, Casca, you and I will yet ere day
See Brutus at his house: three parts of him
Is ours already, and the man entire
Upon the next encounter yields him ours.

CASCA

O, he sits high in all the people's hearts;
And that which would appear offence in us,
His countenance, like richest alchemy,
160 Will change to virtue and to worthiness.

CASSIUS

Him and his worth and our great need of him
You have right well conceited. Let us go,

For it is after midnight, and ere day
We will awake him, and be sure of him.   *Exeunt*

*

Enter Brutus in his orchard

BRUTUS What, Lucius, ho!
I cannot, by the progress of the stars,
Give guess how near to day. Lucius, I say!
I would it were my fault to sleep so soundly.
When, Lucius, when? Awake, I say! What, Lucius!
    Enter Lucius
LUCIUS Called you, my lord?
BRUTUS
Get me a taper in my study, Lucius;
When it is lighted, come and call me here.
LUCIUS I will, my lord.   *Exit*
BRUTUS
It must be by his death; and for my part,   10
I know no personal cause to spurn at him,
But for the general. – He would be crowned.
How that might change his nature, there's the question.
It is the bright day that brings forth the adder,
And that craves wary walking. Crown him! – that!
And then, I grant, we put a sting in him
That at his will he may do danger with.
Th'abuse of greatness is when it disjoins
Remorse from power; and, to speak truth of Caesar,
I have not known when his affections swayed   20
More than his reason. But 'tis a common proof,
That lowliness is young ambition's ladder,
Whereto the climber-upward turns his face;

But when he once attains the upmost round,
He then unto the ladder turns his back,
Looks in the clouds, scorning the base degrees
By which he did ascend: so Caesar may;
Then, lest he may, prevent. And, since the quarrel
Will bear no colour for the thing he is,
30 Fashion it thus: that what he is, augmented,
Would run to these and these extremities;
And therefore think him as a serpent's egg
Which, hatched, would, as his kind, grow mischievous,
And kill him in the shell.

Enter Lucius

LUCIUS
The taper burneth in your closet, sir.
Searching the window for a flint, I found
This paper, thus sealed up; and I am sure
It did not lie there when I went to bed.

He gives him the letter

BRUTUS
Get you to bed again, it is not day.
40 Is not tomorrow, boy, the ides of March?
LUCIUS I know not, sir.
BRUTUS
Look in the calendar and bring me word.
LUCIUS I will, sir. *Exit*
BRUTUS
The exhalations, whizzing in the air,
Give so much light that I may read by them.

He opens the letter and reads

Brutus, thou sleep'st: awake, and see thyself.
Shall Rome, etc. Speak, strike, redress.
'Brutus, thou sleep'st: awake.'
Such instigations have been often dropped

72

Where I have took them up.   50
'Shall Rome, etc.' Thus must I piece it out:
Shall Rome stand under one man's awe? What, Rome?
My ancestors did from the streets of Rome
The Tarquin drive, when he was called a king.
'Speak, strike, redress.' Am I entreated
To speak and strike? O Rome, I make thee promise,
If the redress will follow, thou receivest
Thy full petition at the hand of Brutus.
        Enter Lucius

LUCIUS
    Sir, March is wasted fifteen days.
        Knock within

BRUTUS
    'Tis good. Go to the gate; somebody knocks. *Exit Lucius* 60
    Since Cassius first did whet me against Caesar,
    I have not slept.
    Between the acting of a dreadful thing
    And the first motion, all the interim is
    Like a phantasma or a hideous dream:
    The genius and the mortal instruments
    Are then in council; and the state of man,
    Like to a little kingdom, suffers then
    The nature of an insurrection.
        Enter Lucius

LUCIUS
    Sir, 'tis your brother Cassius at the door,   70
    Who doth desire to see you.

BRUTUS   Is he alone?

LUCIUS
    No, sir, there are more with him.

BRUTUS   Do you know them?

LUCIUS
    No, sir, their hats are plucked about their ears,

73

And half their faces buried in their cloaks,
That by no means I may discover them
By any mark of favour.

BRUTUS   Let 'em enter.   *Exit Lucius*

They are the faction. O conspiracy,
Sham'st thou to show thy dangerous brow by night,
When evils are most free? O then, by day
80 Where wilt thou find a cavern dark enough
To mask thy monstrous visage? Seek none, conspiracy;
Hide it in smiles and affability:
For if thou path, thy native semblance on,
Not Erebus itself were dim enough
To hide thee from prevention.

    Enter the conspirators: Cassius, Casca, Decius, Cinna,
    Metellus, and Trebonius

CASSIUS
I think we are too bold upon your rest.
Good morrow, Brutus; do we trouble you?

BRUTUS
I have been up this hour, awake all night.
Know I these men that come along with you?

CASSIUS
90 Yes, every man of them; and no man here
But honours you; and every one doth wish
You had but that opinion of yourself
Which every noble Roman bears of you.
This is Trebonius.

BRUTUS   He is welcome hither.

CASSIUS
This, Decius Brutus.

BRUTUS   He is welcome too.

CASSIUS
This, Casca; this, Cinna; and this, Metellus Cimber.

BRUTUS They are all welcome.

What watchful cares do interpose themselves
Betwixt your eyes and night?

CASSIUS Shall I entreat a word? 100

They whisper apart

DECIUS

Here lies the east; doth not the day break here?

CASCA No.

CINNA

O pardon, sir, it doth; and yon grey lines
That fret the clouds are messengers of day.

CASCA

You shall confess that you are both deceived:
Here, as I point my sword, the sun arises,
Which is a great way growing on the south,
Weighing the youthful season of the year.
Some two months hence, up higher toward the north
He first presents his fire; and the high east 110
Stands, as the Capitol, directly here.

BRUTUS

Give me your hands all over, one by one.

CASSIUS

And let us swear our resolution.

BRUTUS

No, not an oath. If not the face of men,
The sufferance of our souls, the time's abuse –
If these be motives weak, break off betimes,
And every man hence to his idle bed;
So let high-sighted tyranny range on
Till each man drop by lottery. But if these,
As I am sure they do, bear fire enough 120
To kindle cowards and to steel with valour
The melting spirits of women, then, countrymen,
What need we any spur but our own cause
To prick us to redress? What other bond

75

Than secret Romans that have spoke the word,
And will not palter? And what other oath
Than honesty to honesty engaged
That this shall be, or we will fall for it?
Swear priests and cowards and men cautelous,
130 Old feeble carrions, and such suffering souls
That welcome wrongs; unto bad causes swear
Such creatures as men doubt; but do not stain
The even virtue of our enterprise,
Nor th'insuppressive mettle of our spirits,
To think that or our cause or our performance
Did need an oath; when every drop of blood
That every Roman bears, and nobly bears,
Is guilty of a several bastardy,
If he do break the smallest particle
140 Of any promise that hath passed from him.

CASSIUS

But what of Cicero? Shall we sound him?
I think he will stand very strong with us.

CASCA

Let us not leave him out.

CINNA   No, by no means.

METELLUS

O, let us have him, for his silver hairs
Will purchase us a good opinion
And buy men's voices to commend our deeds.
It shall be said his judgement ruled our hands;
Our youths and wildness shall no whit appear,
But all be buried in his gravity.

BRUTUS

150 O, name him not; let us not break with him,
For he will never follow anything
That other men begin.

CASSIUS   Then leave him out.

76

CASCA Indeed he is not fit.

DECIUS

Shall no man else be touched but only Caesar?

CASSIUS

Decius, well urged. I think it is not meet
Mark Antony, so well beloved of Caesar,
Should outlive Caesar. We shall find of him
A shrewd contriver; and you know his means,
If he improve them, may well stretch so far
As to annoy us all; which to prevent,   160
Let Antony and Caesar fall together.

BRUTUS

Our course will seem too bloody, Caius Cassius,
To cut the head off and then hack the limbs,
Like wrath in death, and envy afterwards;
For Antony is but a limb of Caesar.
Let us be sacrificers, but not butchers, Caius.
We all stand up against the spirit of Caesar,
And in the spirit of men there is no blood.
O, that we then could come by Caesar's spirit,
And not dismember Caesar! But, alas,   170
Caesar must bleed for it. And, gentle friends,
Let's kill him boldly, but not wrathfully;
Let's carve him as a dish fit for the gods,
Not hew him as a carcass fit for hounds.
And let our hearts, as subtle masters do,
Stir up their servants to an act of rage,
And after seem to chide 'em. This shall make
Our purpose necessary, and not envious;
Which so appearing to the common eyes,
We shall be called purgers, not murderers.   180
And for Mark Antony, think not of him;
For he can do no more than Caesar's arm
When Caesar's head is off.

77

CASSIUS   Yet I fear him;
  For in the ingrafted love he bears to Caesar —
BRUTUS
  Alas, good Cassius, do not think of him.
  If he love Caesar, all that he can do
  Is to himself: take thought, and die for Caesar;
  And that were much he should; for he is given
  To sports, to wildness, and much company.
TREBONIUS
190 There is no fear in him; let him not die;
  For he will live, and laugh at this hereafter.
      A clock strikes
BRUTUS
  Peace, count the clock.
CASSIUS   The clock hath stricken three.
TREBONIUS
  'Tis time to part.
CASSIUS   But it is doubtful yet
  Whether Caesar will come forth today or no;
  For he is superstitious grown of late,
  Quite from the main opinion he held once
  Of fantasy, of dreams, and ceremonies.
  It may be these apparent prodigies,
  The unaccustomed terror of this night,
200 And the persuasion of his augurers
  May hold him from the Capitol today.
DECIUS
  Never fear that. If he be so resolved,
  I can o'ersway him; for he loves to hear
  That unicorns may be betrayed with trees,
  And bears with glasses, elephants with holes,
  Lions with toils, and men with flatterers.
  But when I tell him he hates flatterers,
  He says he does, being then most flatterèd.

Let me work;
For I can give his humour the true bent,   210
And I will bring him to the Capitol.

CASSIUS

Nay, we will all of us be there to fetch him.

BRUTUS

By the eighth hour; is that the uttermost?

CINNA

Be that the uttermost, and fail not then.

METELLUS

Caius Ligarius doth bear Caesar hard,
Who rated him for speaking well of Pompey;
I wonder none of you have thought of him.

BRUTUS

Now, good Metellus, go along by him;
He loves me well, and I have given him reasons.
Send him but hither, and I'll fashion him.   220

CASSIUS

The morning comes upon's; we'll leave you, Brutus.
And, friends, disperse yourselves; but all remember
What you have said, and show yourselves true Romans.

BRUTUS

Good gentlemen, look fresh and merrily;
Let not our looks put on our purposes,
But bear it as our Roman actors do,
With untired spirits and formal constancy.
And so good morrow to you every one.

                                Exeunt the conspirators

    Brutus remains
Boy! Lucius! Fast asleep? It is no matter.
Enjoy the honey-heavy dew of slumber;   230
Thou hast no figures nor no fantasies,
Which busy care draws in the brains of men;
Therefore thou sleep'st so sound.

Enter Portia

PORTIA   Brutus, my lord.

BRUTUS

Portia! What mean you? Wherefore rise you now?
It is not for your health thus to commit
Your weak condition to the raw cold morning.

PORTIA

Nor for yours neither. Y' have ungently, Brutus,
Stole from my bed; and yesternight at supper
You suddenly arose and walked about,
240   Musing and sighing, with your arms across;
And when I asked you what the matter was,
You stared upon me with ungentle looks.
I urged you further; then you scratched your head,
And too impatiently stamped with your foot;
Yet I insisted, yet you answered not,
But with an angry wafture of your hand
Gave sign for me to leave you. So I did,
Fearing to strengthen that impatience
Which seemed too much enkindled, and withal
250   Hoping it was but an effect of humour,
Which sometime hath his hour with every man.
It will not let you eat, nor talk, nor sleep;
And could it work so much upon your shape,
As it hath much prevailed on your condition,
I should not know you Brutus. Dear my lord,
Make me acquainted with your cause of grief.

BRUTUS

I am not well in health, and that is all.

PORTIA

Brutus is wise, and were he not in health,
He would embrace the means to come by it.

BRUTUS

260   Why, so I do. Good Portia, go to bed.

PORTIA

   Is Brutus sick? And is it physical
To walk unbracèd and suck up the humours
Of the dank morning? What, is Brutus sick?
And will he steal out of his wholesome bed
To dare the vile contagion of the night,
And tempt the rheumy and unpurgèd air,
To add unto his sickness? No, my Brutus;
You have some sick offence within your mind,
Which, by the right and virtue of my place,
I ought to know of; and, upon my knees,   270
I charm you, by my once commended beauty,
By all your vows of love, and that great vow
Which did incorporate and make us one,
That you unfold to me, your self, your half,
Why you are heavy, and what men tonight
Have had resort to you; for here have been
Some six or seven, who did hide their faces
Even from darkness.

BRUTUS   Kneel not, gentle Portia.

PORTIA

   I should not need, if you were gentle Brutus.
Within the bond of marriage, tell me, Brutus,   280
Is it excepted I should know no secrets
That appertain to you? Am I your self
But, as it were, in sort or limitation,
To keep with you at meals, comfort your bed,
And talk to you sometimes? Dwell I but in the suburbs
Of your good pleasure? If it be no more,
Portia is Brutus' harlot, not his wife.

BRUTUS

   You are my true and honourable wife,
As dear to me as are the ruddy drops
That visit my sad heart.   290

PORTIA

If this were true, then should I know this secret.
I grant I am a woman; but withal
A woman that Lord Brutus took to wife;
I grant I am a woman; but withal
A woman well reputed, Cato's daughter.
Think you I am no stronger than my sex,
Being so fathered, and so husbanded?
Tell me your counsels, I will not disclose 'em.
I have made strong proof of my constancy,
300 Giving myself a voluntary wound
Here, in the thigh; can I bear that with patience,
And not my husband's secrets?

BRUTUS   O ye gods,

Render me worthy of this noble wife!

        Knocking

Hark, hark! one knocks. Portia, go in awhile;
And by and by thy bosom shall partake
The secrets of my heart.
All my engagements I will construe to thee,
All the charactery of my sad brows.
Leave me with haste.   *Exit Portia*

        Enter Lucius and Ligarius

                        Lucius, who's that knocks?

LUCIUS

310 Here is a sick man that would speak with you.

BRUTUS

Caius Ligarius, that Metellus spake of.
Boy, stand aside. Caius Ligarius, how?

LIGARIUS

Vouchsafe good morrow from a feeble tongue.

BRUTUS

O, what a time have you chose out, brave Caius,
To wear a kerchief! Would you were not sick!

LIGARIUS

I am not sick if Brutus have in hand
Any exploit worthy the name of honour.

BRUTUS

Such an exploit have I in hand, Ligarius,
Had you a healthful ear to hear of it.

LIGARIUS

By all the gods that Romans bow before,   320
I here discard my sickness.

   He throws off the kerchief

        Soul of Rome!
Brave son, derived from honourable loins!
Thou, like an exorcist, hast conjured up
My mortifièd spirit. Now bid me run,
And I will strive with things impossible,
Yea, get the better of them. What's to do?

BRUTUS

A piece of work that will make sick men whole.

LIGARIUS

But are not some whole that we must make sick?

BRUTUS

That must we also. What it is, my Caius,
I shall unfold to thee, as we are going   330
To whom it must be done.

LIGARIUS

       Set on your foot,
And with a heart new-fired I follow you,
To do I know not what; but it sufficeth
That Brutus leads me on.

   Thunder

BRUTUS

      Follow me then.   *Exeunt*

Thunder and lightning
Enter Julius Caesar in his night-gown

CAESAR

Nor heaven nor earth have been at peace tonight;
Thrice hath Calphurnia in her sleep cried out,
'Help, ho! They murder Caesar!' Who's within?
Enter a Servant

SERVANT My lord?

CAESAR

Go bid the priests do present sacrifice,
And bring me their opinions of success.

SERVANT I will, my lord.   *Exit*
Enter Calphurnia

CALPHURNIA

What mean you, Caesar? Think you to walk forth?
You shall not stir out of your house today.

CAESAR

10 Caesar shall forth. The things that threatened me
Ne'er looked but on my back; when they shall see
The face of Caesar, they are vanishèd.

CALPHURNIA

Caesar, I never stood on ceremonies,
Yet now they fright me. There is one within,
Besides the things that we have heard and seen,
Recounts most horrid sights seen by the watch.
A lioness hath whelpèd in the streets,
And graves have yawned and yielded up their dead;
Fierce fiery warriors fought upon the clouds
20 In ranks and squadrons and right form of war,
Which drizzled blood upon the Capitol;
The noise of battle hurtled in the air,
Horses did neigh, and dying men did groan,
And ghosts did shriek and squeal about the streets.
O Caesar, these things are beyond all use,

And I do fear them.

CAESAR   What can be avoided

Whose end is purposed by the mighty gods?
Yet Caesar shall go forth; for these predictions
Are to the world in general as to Caesar.

CALPHURNIA

When beggars die, there are no comets seen;   30
The heavens themselves blaze forth the death of princes.

CAESAR

Cowards die many times before their deaths;
The valiant never taste of death but once.
Of all the wonders that I yet have heard,
It seems to me most strange that men should fear,
Seeing that death, a necessary end,
Will come when it will come.

    Enter a Servant

                              What say the augurers?

SERVANT

They would not have you to stir forth today.
Plucking the entrails of an offering forth,
They could not find a heart within the beast.   40

CAESAR

The gods do this in shame of cowardice:
Caesar should be a beast without a heart
If he should stay at home today for fear.
No, Caesar shall not. Danger knows full well
That Caesar is more dangerous than he.
We are two lions littered in one day,
And I the elder and more terrible;
And Caesar shall go forth.

CALPHURNIA   Alas, my lord,

Your wisdom is consumed in confidence.
Do not go forth today: call it my fear   50
That keeps you in the house, and not your own.

We'll send Mark Antony to the Senate House,
And he shall say you are not well today.
Let me upon my knee prevail in this.

CAESAR

Mark Antony shall say I am not well,
And for thy humour I will stay at home.
    Enter Decius
Here's Decius Brutus; he shall tell them so.

DECIUS

Caesar, all hail! Good morrow, worthy Caesar;
I come to fetch you to the Senate House.

CAESAR

60 And you are come in very happy time
To bear my greeting to the senators,
And tell them that I will not come today:
Cannot, is false; and that I dare not, falser;
I will not come today. Tell them so, Decius.

CALPHURNIA

Say he is sick.

CAESAR   Shall Caesar send a lie?
Have I in conquest stretched mine arm so far,
To be afeard to tell greybeards the truth?
Decius, go tell them Caesar will not come.

DECIUS

Most mighty Caesar, let me know some cause,
70 Lest I be laughed at when I tell them so.

CAESAR

The cause is in my will: I will not come;
That is enough to satisfy the Senate.
But for your private satisfaction,
Because I love you, I will let you know:
Calphurnia here, my wife, stays me at home.
She dreamt tonight she saw my statue,
Which, like a fountain with an hundred spouts,

86

Did run pure blood; and many lusty Romans
Came smiling, and did bathe their hands in it.
And these does she apply for warnings and portents   80
And evils imminent; and on her knee
Hath begged that I will stay at home today.

DECIUS

This dream is all amiss interpreted;
It was a vision fair and fortunate:
Your statue spouting blood in many pipes,
In which so many smiling Romans bathed,
Signifies that from you great Rome shall suck
Reviving blood, and that great men shall press
For tinctures, stains, relics, and cognizance.
This by Calphurnia's dream is signified.   90

CAESAR

And this way have you well expounded it.

DECIUS

I have, when you have heard what I can say:
And know it now. The Senate have concluded
To give this day a crown to mighty Caesar.
If you shall send them word you will not come,
Their minds may change. Besides, it were a mock
Apt to be rendered, for some one to say,
'Break up the Senate till another time,
When Caesar's wife shall meet with better dreams.'
If Caesar hide himself, shall they not whisper,   100
'Lo, Caesar is afraid'?
Pardon me, Caesar, for my dear dear love
To your proceeding bids me tell you this,
And reason to my love is liable.

CAESAR

How foolish do your fears seem now, Calphurnia!
I am ashamèd I did yield to them.
Give me my robe, for I will go.

*Enter Brutus, Ligarius, Metellus, Casca, Trebonius,
Cinna, and Publius*

And look where Publius is come to fetch me.

PUBLIUS

Good morrow, Caesar.

CAESAR   Welcome, Publius.

110 What, Brutus, are you stirred so early too?
Good morrow, Casca. Caius Ligarius,
Caesar was ne'er so much your enemy
As that same ague which hath made you lean.
What is't o'clock?

BRUTUS   Caesar, 'tis strucken eight.

CAESAR

I thank you for your pains and courtesy.

Enter Antony

See! Antony, that revels long a-nights,
Is notwithstanding up. Good morrow, Antony.

ANTONY

So to most noble Caesar.

CAESAR   Bid them prepare within.
I am to blame to be thus waited for.

120 Now, Cinna; now, Metellus; what, Trebonius;
I have an hour's talk in store for you;
Remember that you call on me today;
Be near me, that I may remember you.

TREBONIUS

Caesar, I will. (*Aside*) And so near will I be
That your best friends shall wish I had been further.

CAESAR

Good friends, go in, and taste some wine with me;
And we, like friends, will straightway go together.

BRUTUS (*aside*)

That every like is not the same, O Caesar,
The heart of Brutus earns to think upon.   *Exeunt*

Enter Artemidorus reading a paper

ARTEMIDORUS *Caesar, beware of Brutus; take heed of Cassius; come not near Casca; have an eye to Cinna; trust not Trebonius; mark well Metellus Cimber; Decius Brutus loves thee not; thou hast wronged Caius Ligarius. There is but one mind in all these men, and it is bent against Caesar. If thou beest not immortal, look about you: security gives way to conspiracy. The mighty gods defend thee!*

>   *Thy lover,*
>   *Artemidorus.*

Here will I stand till Caesar pass along,   10
And as a suitor will I give him this.
My heart laments that virtue cannot live
Out of the teeth of emulation.
If thou read this, O Caesar, thou mayst live;
If not, the Fates with traitors do contrive.

>   *Exit*

Enter Portia and Lucius

PORTIA
I prithee, boy, run to the Senate House.
Stay not to answer me, but get thee gone.
Why dost thou stay?
LUCIUS   To know my errand, madam.
PORTIA
I would have had thee there and here again
Ere I can tell thee what thou shouldst do there.
O constancy, be strong upon my side;
Set a huge mountain 'tween my heart and tongue!
I have a man's mind, but a woman's might.
How hard it is for women to keep counsel!
Art thou here yet?

10 LUCIUS   Madam, what should I do?
    Run to the Capitol and nothing else?
    And so return to you, and nothing else?

PORTIA
    Yes, bring me word, boy, if thy lord look well,
    For he went sickly forth; and take good note
    What Caesar doth, what suitors press to him.
    Hark, boy, what noise is that?

LUCIUS
    I hear none, madam.

PORTIA   Prithee, listen well.
    I heard a bustling rumour like a fray,
    And the wind brings it from the Capitol.

20 LUCIUS Sooth, madam, I hear nothing.

Enter the Soothsayer

PORTIA
    Come hither fellow. Which way hast thou been?

SOOTHSAYER At mine own house, good lady.

PORTIA
    What is't o'clock?

SOOTHSAYER   About the ninth hour, lady.

PORTIA
    Is Caesar yet gone to the Capitol?

SOOTHSAYER
    Madam, not yet; I go to take my stand,
    To see him pass on to the Capitol.

PORTIA
    Thou hast some suit to Caesar, hast thou not?

SOOTHSAYER
    That I have, lady, if it will please Caesar
    To be so good to Caesar as to hear me:
30 I shall beseech him to befriend himself.

PORTIA
    Why, know'st thou any harm's intended towards him?

SOOTHSAYER

    None that I know will be, much that I fear may chance.
    Good morrow to you. Here the street is narrow;
    The throng that follows Caesar at the heels,
    Of senators, of praetors, common suitors,
    Will crowd a feeble man almost to death;
    I'll get me to a place more void, and there
    Speak to great Caesar as he comes along.   *Exit*

PORTIA

    I must go in. Ay me, how weak a thing
    The heart of woman is! O Brutus,   40
    The heavens speed thee in thine enterprise!
    (*Aside*) Sure, the boy heard me. (*To Lucius*) Brutus hath
        a suit
    That Caesar will not grant. (*Aside*) O, I grow faint.
    Run, Lucius, and commend me to my lord;
    Say I am merry; come to me again,
    And bring me word what he doth say to thee.   *Exeunt*

                    ✳

          Flourish   III.1
          Enter Caesar, Brutus, Cassius, Casca, Decius, Metel-
          lus, Trebonius, Cinna, Antony, Lepidus, Popilius,
          Artemidorus, Publius, and the Soothsayer

CAESAR (*to the Soothsayer*) The ides of March are come.
SOOTHSAYER Ay, Caesar, but not gone.
ARTEMIDORUS Hail, Caesar! Read this schedule.
DECIUS

    Trebonius doth desire you to o'er-read,
    At your best leisure, this his humble suit.

ARTEMIDORUS

    O Caesar, read mine first; for mine's a suit

                    91

That touches Caesar nearer. Read it, great Caesar.

CAESAR

What touches us ourself shall be last served.

ARTEMIDORUS

Delay not, Caesar. Read it instantly.

CAESAR

10   What, is the fellow mad?

PUBLIUS   Sirrah, give place.

CASSIUS

What, urge you your petitions in the street?
Come to the Capitol.

Caesar enters the Capitol, the rest following

POPILIUS

I wish your enterprise today may thrive.

CASSIUS

What enterprise, Popilius?

POPILIUS   Fare you well.

He goes to speak to Caesar

BRUTUS What said Popilius Lena?

CASSIUS

He wished today our enterprise might thrive.
I fear our purpose is discoverèd.

BRUTUS

Look how he makes to Caesar: mark him.

CASSIUS

Casca, be sudden, for we fear prevention.

20   Brutus, what shall be done? If this be known,
Cassius or Caesar never shall turn back,
For I will slay myself.

BRUTUS   Cassius, be constant:
Popilius Lena speaks not of our purposes;
For look, he smiles, and Caesar doth not change.

CASSIUS

Trebonius knows his time; for look you, Brutus,

He draws Mark Antony out of the way.
Exeunt Antony and Trebonius

DECIUS

Where is Metellus Cimber? Let him go,
And presently prefer his suit to Caesar.

BRUTUS

He is addressed. Press near and second him.

CINNA

Casca, you are the first that rears your hand.   30

CAESAR

Are we all ready? What is now amiss
That Caesar and his senate must redress?

METELLUS (*kneeling*)

Most high, most mighty, and most puissant Caesar,
Metellus Cimber throws before thy seat
An humble heart –

CAESAR   I must prevent thee, Cimber;
These couchings, and these lowly courtesies
Might fire the blood of ordinary men,
And turn pre-ordinance and first decree
Into the law of children. Be not fond,
To think that Caesar bears such rebel blood   40
That will be thawed from the true quality
With that which melteth fools – I mean sweet words,
Low-crookèd curtsies and base spaniel fawning.
Thy brother by decree is banishèd:
If thou dost bend and pray and fawn for him,
I spurn thee like a cur out of my way.
Know, Caesar doth not wrong, nor without cause
Will he be satisfied.

METELLUS

Is there no voice more worthy than my own,
To sound more sweetly in great Caesar's ear   50
For the repealing of my banished brother?

93

BRUTUS

  I kiss thy hand, but not in flattery, Caesar,
  Desiring thee that Publius Cimber may
  Have an immediate freedom of repeal.

CAESAR What, Brutus?

CASSIUS (*kneeling*)   Pardon, Caesar; Caesar, pardon;
  As low as to thy foot doth Cassius fall,
  To beg enfranchisement for Publius Cimber.

CAESAR

  I could be well moved, if I were as you;
  If I could pray to move, prayers would move me;
60 But I am constant as the northern star,
  Of whose true-fixed and resting quality
  There is no fellow in the firmament—*heaven*
  The skies are painted with unnumbered sparks,
  They are all fire, and every one doth shine;
  But there's but one in all doth hold his place.
  So in the world: 'tis furnished well with men,
  And men are flesh and blood, and apprehensive;
  Yet in the number I do know but one
  That unassailable holds on his rank,
70 Unshaked of motion; and that I am he,
  Let me a little show it, even in this:
  That I was constant Cimber should be banished,
  And constant do remain to keep him so.

CINNA

  O Caesar –

CAESAR   Hence! Wilt thou lift up Olympus?

DECIUS

  Great Caesar –

CAESAR   Doth not Brutus bootless kneel?

CASCA Speak hands for me!

    They stab Caesar

Brutus hesitates

CAESAR

   Et tu, Brute? – Then fall Caesar!   *He dies*

CINNA

   Liberty! Freedom! Tyranny is dead!
   Run hence, proclaim, cry it about the streets.

CASSIUS

   Some to the common pulpits, and cry out,   80
   'Liberty, freedom, and enfranchisement!'

BRUTUS

   People and senators, be not affrighted.
   Fly not; stand still; ambition's debt is paid.

CASCA   CAESAR

   Go to the pulpit, Brutus.

DECIUS   And Cassius too.

BRUTUS Where's Publius?

CINNA

   Here, quite confounded with this mutiny.

METELLUS

   Stand fast together, lest some friend of Caesar's
   Should chance –

BRUTUS

   Talk not of standing. Publius, good cheer;
   There is no harm intended to your person,   90
   Nor to no Roman else. So tell them, Publius.

CASSIUS

   And leave us, Publius, lest that the people,
   Rushing on us, should do your age some mischief.

BRUTUS

   Do so; and let no man abide this deed
   But we the doers.

     Enter Trebonius

CASSIUS

   Where is Antony?

TREBONIUS   Fled to his house amazed.
Men, wives, and children stare, cry out, and run,
As it were doomsday.
BRUTUS   Fates, we will know your pleasures.
That we shall die, we know; 'tis but the time
100 And drawing days out, that men stand upon.
CASCA
Why, he that cuts off twenty years of life
Cuts off so many years of fearing death.
BRUTUS
Grant that, and then is death a benefit:
So are we Caesar's friends, that have abridged
His time of fearing death. Stoop, Romans, stoop,
And let us bathe our hands in Caesar's blood
Up to the elbows, and besmear our swords;
Then walk we forth, even to the market-place,
And waving our red weapons o'er our heads,
110 Let's all cry, 'Peace, freedom, and liberty!'
CASSIUS
Stoop then, and wash. How many ages hence
Shall this our lofty scene be acted over,
In states unborn, and accents yet unknown!
BRUTUS
How many times shall Caesar bleed in sport,
That now on Pompey's basis lies along,
No worthier than the dust!
CASSIUS   So oft as that shall be,
So often shall the knot of us be called
The men that gave their country liberty.
DECIUS
What, shall we forth?
CASSIUS   Ay, every man away.
120 Brutus shall lead, and we will grace his heels
With the most boldest and best hearts of Rome.

Enter a Servant

BRUTUS

Soft, who comes here? A friend of Antony's.

SERVANT (*kneeling*)

Thus, Brutus, did my master bid me kneel;
Thus did Mark Antony bid me fall down;
And, being prostrate, thus he bade me say:
Brutus is noble, wise, valiant, and honest;
Caesar was mighty, bold, royal, and loving:
Say I love Brutus, and I honour him;
Say I feared Caesar, honoured him, and loved him.
If Brutus will vouchsafe that Antony   130
May safely come to him, and be resolved
How Caesar hath deserved to lie in death,
Mark Antony shall not love Caesar dead
So well as Brutus living; but will follow
The fortunes and affairs of noble Brutus
Thorough the hazards of this untrod state,
With all true faith. So says my master Antony.

BRUTUS

Thy master is a wise and valiant Roman;
I never thought him worse.
Tell him, so please him come unto this place,   140
He shall be satisfied; and, by my honour,
Depart untouched.

SERVANT   I'll fetch him presently.

Exit Servant

BRUTUS

I know that we shall have him well to friend.

CASSIUS

I wish we may: but yet have I a mind
That fears him much; and my misgiving still
Falls shrewdly to the purpose.

Enter Antony

BRUTUS

But here comes Antony. Welcome, Mark Antony.

ANTONY

O mighty Caesar! Dost thou lie so low?
Are all thy conquests, glories, triumphs, spoils
150 Shrunk to this little measure? Fare thee well.
I know not, gentlemen, what you intend,
Who else must be let blood, who else is rank:
If I myself, there is no hour so fit
As Caesar's death's hour; nor no instrument
Of half that worth as those your swords, made rich
With the most noble blood of all this world.
I do beseech ye, if you bear me hard,
Now, whilst your purpled hands do reek and smoke,
Fulfil your pleasure. Live a thousand years,
160 I shall not find myself so apt to die;
No place will please me so, no mean of death,
As here by Caesar, and by you cut off,
The choice and master spirits of this age.

BRUTUS

O Antony, beg not your death of us.
Though now we must appear bloody and cruel,
As by our hands and this our present act
You see we do, yet see you but our hands
And this the bleeding business they have done.
Our hearts you see not; they are pitiful;
170 And pity to the general wrong of Rome –
As fire drives out fire, so pity, pity –
Hath done this deed on Caesar. For your part,
To you our swords have leaden points, Mark Antony;
Our arms in strength of malice, and our hearts
Of brothers' temper, do receive you in
With all kind love, good thoughts, and reverence.

CASSIUS

    Your voice shall be as strong as any man's
    In the disposing of new dignities.

BRUTUS

    Only be patient till we have appeased
    The multitude, beside themselves with fear,   180
    And then we will deliver you the cause
    Why I, that did love Caesar when I struck him,
    Have thus proceeded.

ANTONY   I doubt not of your wisdom.
    Let each man render me his bloody hand.
    First, Marcus Brutus, will I shake with you;
    Next, Caius Cassius, do I take your hand;
    Now, Decius Brutus, yours; now yours, Metellus;
    Yours, Cinna; and, my valiant Casca, yours;
    Though last, not least in love, yours, good Trebonius.
    Gentlemen all – alas, what shall I say?   190
    My credit now stands on such slippery ground,
    That one of two bad ways you must conceit me,
    Either a coward, or a flatterer.
    That I did love thee, Caesar, O, 'tis true!
    If then thy spirit look upon us now,
    Shall it not grieve thee dearer than thy death,
    To see thy Antony making his peace,
    Shaking the bloody fingers of thy foes,
    Most noble, in the presence of thy corse?
    Had I as many eyes as thou hast wounds,   200
    Weeping as fast as they stream forth thy blood,
    It would become me better than to close
    In terms of friendship with thine enemies.
    Pardon me, Julius! Here wast thou bayed, brave hart;
    Here didst thou fall; and here thy hunters stand,
    Signed in thy spoil, and crimsoned in thy lethe.
    O world, thou wast the forest to this hart;

And this indeed, O world, the heart of thee.
How like a deer, strucken by many princes,
210 Dost thou here lie!

CASSIUS
Mark Antony –

ANTONY   Pardon me, Caius Cassius;
The enemies of Caesar shall say this;
Then, in a friend, it is cold modesty.

CASSIUS
I blame you not for praising Caesar so;
But what compact mean you to have with us?
Will you be pricked in number of our friends,
Or shall we on, and not depend on you?

ANTONY
Therefore I took your hands, but was indeed
Swayed from the point by looking down on Caesar.
220 Friends am I with you all, and love you all,
Upon this hope, that you shall give me reasons
Why, and wherein, Caesar was dangerous.

BRUTUS
Or else were this a savage spectacle.
Our reasons are so full of good regard,
That were you, Antony, the son of Caesar,
You should be satisfied.

ANTONY   That's all I seek,
And am moreover suitor that I may
Produce his body to the market-place,
And in the pulpit, as becomes a friend,
230 Speak in the order of his funeral.

BRUTUS
You shall, Mark Antony.

CASSIUS   Brutus, a word with you.
(*Aside to Brutus*) You know not what you do; do not
                    consent

100

That Antony speak in his funeral.
Know you how much the people may be moved
By that which he will utter?

BRUTUS (*aside to Cassius*)   By your pardon:
I will myself into the pulpit first,
And show the reason of our Caesar's death.
What Antony shall speak, I will protest
He speaks by leave and by permission;
And that we are contented Caesar shall   240
Have all true rites and lawful ceremonies,
It shall advantage more than do us wrong.

CASSIUS (*aside to Brutus*)
I know not what may fall; I like it not.

BRUTUS
Mark Antony, here take you Caesar's body.
You shall not in your funeral speech blame us,
But speak all good you can devise of Caesar,
And say you do't by our permission;
Else shall you not have any hand at all
About his funeral. And you shall speak
In the same pulpit whereto I am going,   250
After my speech is ended.

ANTONY   Be it so;
I do desire no more.

BRUTUS
Prepare the body, then, and follow us.   *Exeunt*
      Antony remains

ANTONY
O, pardon me, thou bleeding piece of earth,
That I am meek and gentle with these butchers.
Thou art the ruins of the noblest man
That ever livèd in the tide of times.
Woe to the hand that shed this costly blood!
Over thy wounds now do I prophesy –

260   Which like dumb mouths do ope their ruby lips,
      To beg the voice and utterance of my tongue –
      A curse shall light upon the limbs of men;
      Domestic fury and fierce civil strife
      Shall cumber all the parts of Italy;
      Blood and destruction shall be so in use,
      And dreadful objects so familiar,
      That mothers shall but smile when they behold
      Their infants quartered with the hands of war,
      All pity choked with custom of fell deeds;
270   And Caesar's spirit, ranging for revenge,
      With Ate by his side, come hot from hell,
      Shall in these confines with a monarch's voice
      Cry havoc and let slip the dogs of war,
      That this foul deed shall smell above the earth
      With carrion men, groaning for burial.

> *Enter Octavius's Servant*

      You serve Octavius Caesar, do you not?
SERVANT I do, Mark Antony.
ANTONY
      Caesar did write for him to come to Rome.
SERVANT
      He did receive his letters, and is coming,
280   And bid me say to you by word of mouth –
      O Caesar!
ANTONY
      Thy heart is big; get thee apart and weep.
      Passion, I see, is catching, for mine eyes,
      Seeing those beads of sorrow stand in thine,
      Began to water. Is thy master coming?
SERVANT
      He lies tonight within seven leagues of Rome.
ANTONY
      Post back with speed, and tell him what hath chanced.

Here is a mourning Rome, a dangerous Rome,
No Rome of safety for Octavius yet.
Hie hence, and tell him so. Yet stay awhile;   290
Thou shalt not back till I have borne this corse
Into the market-place; there shall I try,
In my oration, how the people take
The cruel issue of these bloody men;
According to the which, thou shalt discourse
To young Octavius of the state of things.
Lend me your hand.   *Exeunt*

Enter Brutus and later goes into the pulpit, and III.2
Cassius, with the Plebeians

PLEBEIANS We will be satisfied: let us be satisfied.
BRUTUS
Then follow me, and give me audience, friends.
Cassius, go you into the other street,
And part the numbers.
Those that will hear me speak, let 'em stay here;
Those that will follow Cassius, go with him;
And public reasons shall be renderèd
Of Caesar's death.
FIRST PLEBEIAN   I will hear Brutus speak.
SECOND PLEBEIAN
I will hear Cassius, and compare their reasons,
When severally we hear them renderèd.   10
Exit Cassius, with some of the Plebeians
THIRD PLEBEIAN
The noble Brutus is ascended. Silence!
BRUTUS Be patient till the last.
Romans, countrymen, and lovers, hear me for my cause,
and be silent, that you may hear. Believe me for mine
honour, and have respect to mine honour, that you may

believe. Censure me in your wisdom, and awake your
senses, that you may the better judge. If there be any in
this assembly, any dear friend of Caesar's, to him I say
that Brutus' love to Caesar was no less than his. If then
that friend demand why Brutus rose against Caesar, this
is my answer: not that I loved Caesar less, but that I
loved Rome more. Had you rather Caesar were living,
and die all slaves, than that Caesar were dead, to live
all free men? As Caesar loved me, I weep for him; as
he was fortunate, I rejoice at it; as he was valiant, I
honour him; but, as he was ambitious, I slew him.
There is tears for his love; joy for his fortune; honour
for his valour; and death for his ambition. Who is here
so base that would be a bondman? If any, speak; for
him have I offended. Who is here so rude that would
not be a Roman? If any, speak; for him have I offended. Who is here so vile that will not love his country?
If any, speak; for him have I offended. I pause for a
reply.

ALL None, Brutus, none.

BRUTUS Then none have I offended. I have done no more
to Caesar than you shall do to Brutus. The question of
his death is enrolled in the Capitol; his glory not extenuated, wherein he was worthy; nor his offences enforced,
for which he suffered death.

Enter Mark Antony and others, with Caesar's body
Here comes his body, mourned by Mark Antony, who,
though he had no hand in his death, shall receive the
benefit of his dying, a place in the commonwealth, as
which of you shall not? With this I depart, that, as I
slew my best lover for the good of Rome, I have the
same dagger for myself, when it shall please my country
to need my death.

ALL Live, Brutus! live! live!

FIRST PLEBEIAN
Bring him with triumph home unto his house.

SECOND PLEBEIAN
Give him a statue with his ancestors.   50

THIRD PLEBEIAN
Let him be Caesar.

FOURTH PLEBEIAN Caesar's better parts
Shall be crowned in Brutus.

FIRST PLEBEIAN
We'll bring him to his house with shouts and clamours.

BRUTUS
My countrymen –

SECOND PLEBEIAN Peace! Silence! Brutus speaks.

FIRST PLEBEIAN Peace, ho!

BRUTUS
Good countrymen, let me depart alone,
And, for my sake, stay here with Antony.
Do grace to Caesar's corpse, and grace his speech
Tending to Caesar's glories, which Mark Antony,
By our permission, is allowed to make.   60
I do entreat you, not a man depart,
Save I alone, till Antony have spoke.   *Exit*

FIRST PLEBEIAN
Stay, ho! and let us hear Mark Antony.

THIRD PLEBEIAN
Let him go up into the public chair;
We'll hear him. Noble Antony, go up.

ANTONY
For Brutus' sake, I am beholding to you.

FOURTH PLEBEIAN
What does he say of Brutus?

THIRD PLEBEIAN   He says, for Brutus' sake
He finds himself beholding to us all.

105

FOURTH PLEBEIAN
'Twere best he speak no harm of Brutus here!

FIRST PLEBEIAN
70   This Caesar was a tyrant.

THIRD PLEBEIAN   Nay, that's certain.
We are blest that Rome is rid of him.

SECOND PLEBEIAN
Peace! let us hear what Antony can say.

ANTONY
You gentle Romans –

SECOND PLEBEIAN   Peace, ho! let us hear him.

ANTONY
Friends, Romans, countrymen, lend me your ears;
I come to bury Caesar, not to praise him.
The evil that men do lives after them,
The good is oft interrèd with their bones;
So let it be with Caesar. The noble Brutus
Hath told you Caesar was ambitious.
80   If it were so, it was a grievous fault,
And grievously hath Caesar answered it.
Here, under leave of Brutus and the rest –
For Brutus is an honourable man;
So are they all, all honourable men –
Come I to speak in Caesar's funeral.
He was my friend, faithful and just to me;
But Brutus says he was ambitious,
And Brutus is an honourable man.
He hath brought many captives home to Rome,
90   Whose ransoms did the general coffers fill:
Did this in Caesar seem ambitious?
When that the poor have cried, Caesar hath wept;
Ambition should be made of sterner stuff:
Yet Brutus says he was ambitious,
And Brutus is an honourable man.

You all did see that on the Lupercal
I thrice presented him a kingly crown,
Which he did thrice refuse. Was this ambition?
Yet Brutus says he was ambitious,
And sure he is an honourable man.   100
I speak not to disprove what Brutus spoke,
But here I am to speak what I do know.
You all did love him once, not without cause;
What cause withholds you then to mourn for him?
O judgement! thou art fled to brutish beasts,
And men have lost their reason. Bear with me;
My heart is in the coffin there with Caesar,
And I must pause till it come back to me.

FIRST PLEBEIAN
Methinks there is much reason in his sayings.

SECOND PLEBEIAN
If thou consider rightly of the matter,   110
Caesar has had great wrong.

THIRD PLEBEIAN   Has he, masters?
I fear there will a worse come in his place.

FOURTH PLEBEIAN
Marked ye his words? He would not take the crown;
Therefore 'tis certain he was not ambitious.

FIRST PLEBEIAN
If it be found so, some will dear abide it.

SECOND PLEBEIAN
Poor soul! His eyes are red as fire with weeping.

THIRD PLEBEIAN
There's not a nobler man in Rome than Antony.

FOURTH PLEBEIAN
Now mark him; he begins again to speak.

ANTONY
But yesterday the word of Caesar might

120 Have stood against the world; now lies he there,
And none so poor to do him reverence.
O masters! If I were disposed to stir
Your hearts and minds to mutiny and rage,
I should do Brutus wrong, and Cassius wrong,
Who, you all know, are honourable men.
I will not do them wrong; I rather choose
To wrong the dead, to wrong myself and you,
Than I will wrong such honourable men.
But here's a parchment with the seal of Caesar;
130 I found it in his closet; 'tis his will.
Let but the commons hear this testament,
Which, pardon me, I do not mean to read,
And they would go and kiss dead Caesar's wounds,
And dip their napkins in his sacred blood,
Yea, beg a hair of him for memory,
And, dying, mention it within their wills,
Bequeathing it as a rich legacy
Unto their issue.

FOURTH PLEBEIAN

We'll hear the will. Read it, Mark Antony.

ALL

140 The will, the will! We will hear Caesar's will!

ANTONY

Have patience, gentle friends; I must not read it.
It is not meet you know how Caesar loved you.
You are not wood, you are not stones, but men;
And being men, hearing the will of Caesar,
It will inflame you, it will make you mad.
'Tis good you know not that you are his heirs;
For if you should, O, what would come of it?

FOURTH PLEBEIAN

Read the will! We'll hear it, Antony!
You shall read us the will, Caesar's will!

ANTONY

Will you be patient? Will you stay awhile? 150
I have o'ershot myself to tell you of it.
I fear I wrong the honourable men
Whose daggers have stabbed Caesar; I do fear it.

FOURTH PLEBEIAN They were traitors. Honourable men!

ALL The will! The testament!

SECOND PLEBEIAN They were villains, murderers! The
will! Read the will!

ANTONY

You will compel me then to read the will?
Then make a ring about the corpse of Caesar,
And let me show you him that made the will. 160
Shall I descend? And will you give me leave?

ALL Come down.

Antony comes down from the pulpit

SECOND PLEBEIAN Descend.

THIRD PLEBEIAN You shall have leave.

FOURTH PLEBEIAN A ring! Stand round.

FIRST PLEBEIAN

Stand from the hearse! Stand from the body!

SECOND PLEBEIAN

Room for Antony, most noble Antony!

ANTONY

Nay, press not so upon me; stand far off.

ALL Stand back! Room! Bear back!

ANTONY

If you have tears, prepare to shed them now. 170
You all do know this mantle. I remember
The first time ever Caesar put it on;
'Twas on a summer's evening in his tent,
That day he overcame the Nervii.
Look, in this place ran Cassius' dagger through;

See what a rent the envious Casca made;
Through this, the well-belovèd Brutus stabbed,
And as he plucked his cursèd steel away,
Mark how the blood of Caesar followed it,
180 As rushing out of doors, to be resolved
If Brutus so unkindly knocked or no;
For Brutus, as you know, was Caesar's angel.
Judge, O you gods, how dearly Caesar loved him!
This was the most unkindest cut of all;
For when the noble Caesar saw him stab,
Ingratitude, more strong than traitors' arms,
Quite vanquished him: then burst his mighty heart;
And in his mantle muffling up his face,
Even at the base of Pompey's statue,
190 Which all the while ran blood, great Caesar fell.
O, what a fall was there, my countrymen!
Then I, and you, and all of us fell down,
Whilst bloody treason flourished over us.
O, now you weep, and I perceive you feel
The dint of pity. These are gracious drops.
Kind souls, what weep you when you but behold
Our Caesar's vesture wounded? Look you here,
Here is himself, marred, as you see, with traitors.

Antony plucks off the mantle

FIRST PLEBEIAN O piteous spectacle!
200 SECOND PLEBEIAN O noble Caesar!
THIRD PLEBEIAN O woeful day!
FOURTH PLEBEIAN O traitors! villains!
FIRST PLEBEIAN O most bloody sight!
SECOND PLEBEIAN We will be revenged.
ALL Revenge! About! Seek! Burn! Fire! Kill! Slay! Let
not a traitor live.
ANTONY Stay, countrymen.
FIRST PLEBEIAN Peace there! Hear the noble Antony!

SECOND PLEBEIAN We'll hear him, we'll follow him, we'll die with him. 210

ANTONY

Good friends, sweet friends, let me not stir you up
To such a sudden flood of mutiny.
They that have done this deed are honourable.
What private griefs they have, alas, I know not,
That made them do it. They are wise and honourable,
And will, no doubt, with reasons answer you.
I come not, friends, to steal away your hearts;
I am no orator, as Brutus is,
But, as you know me all, a plain blunt man,
That love my friend; and that they know full well 220
That gave me public leave to speak of him.
For I have neither wit, nor words, nor worth,
Action, nor utterance, nor the power of speech
To stir men's blood; I only speak right on.
I tell you that which you yourselves do know,
Show you sweet Caesar's wounds, poor poor dumb
        mouths,
And bid them speak for me. But were I Brutus,
And Brutus Antony, there were an Antony
Would ruffle up your spirits, and put a tongue
In every wound of Caesar that should move 230
The stones of Rome to rise and mutiny.

ALL

We'll mutiny.

FIRST PLEBEIAN We'll burn the house of Brutus.

THIRD PLEBEIAN

Away then! Come, seek the conspirators.

ANTONY

Yet hear me, countrymen; yet hear me speak.

ALL Peace, ho! Hear Antony, most noble Antony!

ANTONY

Why, friends, you go to do you know not what.
Wherein hath Caesar thus deserved your loves?
Alas, you know not! I must tell you then:
You have forgot the will I told you of.

ALL

240 Most true. The will! Let's stay and hear the will.

ANTONY

Here is the will, and under Caesar's seal.
To every Roman citizen he gives,
To every several man, seventy-five drachmas.

SECOND PLEBEIAN

Most noble Caesar! We'll revenge his death.

THIRD PLEBEIAN O royal Caesar!

ANTONY Hear me with patience.

ALL Peace, ho!

ANTONY

Moreover, he hath left you all his walks,
His private arbours, and new-planted orchards,
250 On this side Tiber; he hath left them you,
And to your heirs for ever: common pleasures,
To walk abroad and recreate yourselves.
Here was a Caesar! When comes such another?

FIRST PLEBEIAN

Never, never! Come, away, away!
We'll burn his body in the holy place,
And with the brands fire the traitors' houses.
Take up the body.

SECOND PLEBEIAN Go fetch fire.

THIRD PLEBEIAN Pluck down benches.

260 FOURTH PLEBEIAN Pluck down forms, windows, anything.

Exeunt Plebeians with the body

112

ANTONY

Now let it work. Mischief, thou art afoot,
Take thou what course thou wilt.

Enter Servant

How now, fellow?

SERVANT

Sir, Octavius is already come to Rome.

ANTONY Where is he?

SERVANT

He and Lepidus are at Caesar's house.

ANTONY

And thither will I straight to visit him.
He comes upon a wish. Fortune is merry,
And in this mood will give us anything.

SERVANT

I heard him say Brutus and Cassius   270
Are rid like madmen through the gates of Rome.

ANTONY

Belike they had some notice of the people,
How I had moved them. Bring me to Octavius. *Exeunt*

Enter Cinna the Poet, and after him the Plebeians   III.3

CINNA

I dreamt tonight that I did feast with Caesar,
And things unluckily charge my fantasy;
I have no will to wander forth of doors,
Yet something leads me forth.

The Plebeians surround him

FIRST PLEBEIAN What is your name?

SECOND PLEBEIAN Whither are you going?

THIRD PLEBEIAN Where do you dwell?

FOURTH PLEBEIAN Are you a married man or a bachelor?

SECOND PLEBEIAN Answer every man directly.

10 FIRST PLEBEIAN Ay, and briefly.

FOURTH PLEBEIAN Ay, and wisely.

THIRD PLEBEIAN Ay, and truly, you were best.

CINNA What is my name? Whither am I going? Where do I dwell? Am I a married man or a bachelor? Then to answer every man directly and briefly, wisely and truly; wisely I say, I am a bachelor.

SECOND PLEBEIAN That's as much as to say they are fools that marry. You'll bear me a bang for that, I fear. Proceed, directly.

20 CINNA Directly, I am going to Caesar's funeral.

FIRST PLEBEIAN As a friend or an enemy?

CINNA As a friend.

SECOND PLEBEIAN That matter is answered directly.

FOURTH PLEBEIAN For your dwelling, briefly.

CINNA Briefly, I dwell by the Capitol.

THIRD PLEBEIAN Your name, sir, truly.

CINNA Truly, my name is Cinna.

FIRST PLEBEIAN Tear him to pieces! He's a conspirator.

CINNA I am Cinna the poet, I am Cinna the poet.

30 FOURTH PLEBEIAN Tear him for his bad verses, tear him for his bad verses!

CINNA I am not Cinna the conspirator.

FOURTH PLEBEIAN It is no matter, his name's Cinna; pluck but his name out of his heart, and turn him going.

THIRD PLEBEIAN Tear him, tear him!

They attack Cinna

Come, brands, ho, firebrands! To Brutus', to Cassius'; burn all! Some to Decius' house, and some to Casca's; some to Ligarius'. Away, go!

Exeunt all the Plebeians with Cinna's body

*

ANTONY

  These many then shall die; their names are pricked.

OCTAVIUS

  Your brother too must die; consent you, Lepidus?

LEPIDUS

  I do consent.

OCTAVIUS   Prick him down, Antony.

LEPIDUS

  Upon condition Publius shall not live,

  Who is your sister's son, Mark Antony.

ANTONY

  He shall not live. Look, with a spot I damn him.

  But, Lepidus, go you to Caesar's house;

  Fetch the will hither, and we shall determine

  How to cut off some charge in legacies.

LEPIDUS What, shall I find you here?   10

OCTAVIUS Or here or at the Capitol.   *Exit Lepidus*

ANTONY

  This is a slight unmeritable man,

  Meet to be sent on errands. Is it fit,

  The three-fold world divided, he should stand

  One of the three to share it?

OCTAVIUS   So you thought him,

  And took his voice who should be pricked to die

  In our black sentence and proscription.

ANTONY

  Octavius, I have seen more days than you;

  And though we lay these honours on this man,

  To ease ourselves of divers slanderous loads,   20

  He shall but bear them as the ass bears gold,

  To groan and sweat under the business,

  Either led or driven, as we point the way;

  And having brought our treasure where we will,

Then take we down his load, and turn him off,
Like to the empty ass, to shake his ears
And graze in commons.

OCTAVIUS   You may do your will;
But he's a tried and valiant soldier.

ANTONY
So is my horse, Octavius, and for that
30 I do appoint him store of provender.
It is a creature that I teach to fight,
To wind, to stop, to run directly on,
His corporal motion governed by my spirit.
And, in some taste, is Lepidus but so:
He must be taught, and trained, and bid go forth:
A barren-spirited fellow; one that feeds
On objects, arts, and imitations,
Which, out of use and staled by other men,
Begins his fashion. Do not talk of him
40 But as a property. And now, Octavius,
Listen great things. Brutus and Cassius
Are levying powers; we must straight make head.
Therefore let our alliance be combined,
Our best friends made, our means stretched;
And let us presently go sit in council,
How covert matters may be best disclosed,
And open perils surest answerèd.

OCTAVIUS
Let us do so; for we are at the stake,
And bayed about with many enemies;
50 And some that smile have in their hearts, I fear,
Millions of mischiefs.   *Exeunt*

Enter Brutus, Lucilius, Lucius, and the army. Titinius
and Pindarus meet them

BRUTUS Stand, ho!

LUCILIUS Give the word, ho! and stand!

BRUTUS

What now, Lucilius, is Cassius near?

LUCILIUS

He is at hand, and Pindarus is come
To do you salutation from his master.

BRUTUS

He greets me well. Your master, Pindarus,
In his own change, or by ill officers,
Hath given me some worthy cause to wish
Things done undone; but if he be at hand
I shall be satisfied.

PINDARUS   I do not doubt   10
But that my noble master will appear
Such as he is, full of regard and honour.

BRUTUS

He is not doubted. A word, Lucilius;
    Brutus and Lucilius draw apart
How he received you, let me be resolved.

LUCILIUS

With courtesy and with respect enough,
But not with such familiar instances,
Nor with such free and friendly conference,
As he hath used of old.

BRUTUS   Thou hast described
A hot friend cooling. Ever note, Lucilius,
When love begins to sicken and decay,   20
It useth an enforcèd ceremony.
There are no tricks in plain and simple faith;
But hollow men, like horses hot at hand,

Make gallant show and promise of their mettle;
> *Low march within*

But when they should endure the bloody spur,
They fall their crests, and like deceitful jades
Sink in the trial. Comes his army on?

LUCILIUS

They mean this night in Sardis to be quartered;
The greater part, the horse in general,

30 Are come with Cassius.

> *Enter Cassius and his powers*

> > Hark! he is arrived.

March gently on to meet him.

CASSIUS Stand, ho!

BRUTUS Stand, ho! Speak the word along.

FIRST SOLDIER Stand!

SECOND SOLDIER Stand!

THIRD SOLDIER Stand!

CASSIUS

Most noble brother, you have done me wrong.

BRUTUS

Judge me, you gods; wrong I mine enemies?
And if not so, how should I wrong a brother?

CASSIUS

40 Brutus, this sober form of yours hides wrongs;
And when you do them —

BRUTUS   Cassius, be content.
Speak your griefs softly; I do know you well.
Before the eyes of both our armies here,
Which should perceive nothing but love from us,
Let us not wrangle. Bid them move away;
Then in my tent, Cassius, enlarge your griefs,
And I will give you audience.

CASSIUS   Pindarus,
Bid our commanders lead their charges off

A little from this ground.

BRUTUS

    Lucius, do you the like, and let no man   50
    Come to our tent till we have done our conference.
    Lucilius and Titinius guard our door.

Exeunt all except Brutus and Cassius

CASSIUS

    That you have wronged me doth appear in this:
    You have condemned and noted Lucius Pella
    For taking bribes here of the Sardians;
    Wherein my letters, praying on his side,
    Because I knew the man, was slighted off.

BRUTUS

    You wronged yourself to write in such a case.

CASSIUS

    In such a time as this it is not meet
    That every nice offence should bear his comment.

BRUTUS

    Let me tell you, Cassius, you yourself
    Are much condemned to have an itching palm,   10
    To sell and mart your offices for gold
    To undeservers.

CASSIUS   I an itching palm!

    You know that you are Brutus that speaks this,
    Or, by the gods, this speech were else your last.

BRUTUS

    The name of Cassius honours this corruption,
    And chastisement doth therefore hide his head.

CASSIUS Chastisement!

BRUTUS

    Remember March, the ides of March remember.
    Did not great Julius bleed for justice' sake?

20   What villain touched his body, that did stab,
And not for justice? What, shall one of us,
That struck the foremost man of all this world
But for supporting robbers, shall we now
Contaminate our fingers with base bribes,
And sell the mighty space of our large honours
For so much trash as may be graspèd thus?
I had rather be a dog, and bay the moon,
Than such a Roman.

CASSIUS   Brutus, bait not me;
I'll not endure it. You forget yourself,
30   To hedge me in. I am a soldier, I,
Older in practice, abler than yourself
To make conditions.

BRUTUS   Go to! You are not, Cassius.

CASSIUS I am.

BRUTUS I say you are not.

CASSIUS

Urge me no more, I shall forget myself;
Have mind upon your health; tempt me no further.

BRUTUS Away, slight man!

CASSIUS

Is't possible?

BRUTUS   Hear me, for I will speak.
Must I give way and room to your rash choler?
40   Shall I be frighted when a madman stares?

CASSIUS

O ye gods, ye gods! Must I endure all this?

BRUTUS

All this? Ay, more: fret till your proud heart break;
Go show your slaves how choleric you are,
And make your bondmen tremble. Must I budge?
Must I observe you? Must I stand and crouch
Under your testy humour? By the gods,

You shall disgest the venom of your spleen,
Though it do split you; for, from this day forth,
I'll use you for my mirth, yea, for my laughter,
When you are waspish.

CASSIUS   Is it come to this?   50

BRUTUS
You say you are a better soldier:
Let it appear so; make your vaunting true,
And it shall please me well. For mine own part,
I shall be glad to learn of noble men.

CASSIUS
You wrong me every way; you wrong me, Brutus.
I said an elder soldier, not a better;
Did I say better?

BRUTUS   If you did, I care not.

CASSIUS
When Caesar lived, he durst not thus have moved me.

BRUTUS
Peace, peace! You durst not so have tempted him.

CASSIUS I durst not?   60

BRUTUS No.

CASSIUS
What, durst not tempt him?

BRUTUS   For your life you durst not.

CASSIUS
Do not presume too much upon my love;
I may do that I shall be sorry for.

BRUTUS
You have done that you should be sorry for.
There is no terror, Cassius, in your threats;
For I am armed so strong in honesty
That they pass by me as the idle wind,
Which I respect not. I did send to you
For certain sums of gold, which you denied me;   70

For I can raise no money by vile means;
By heaven, I had rather coin my heart,
And drop my blood for drachmas, than to wring
From the hard hands of peasants their vile trash
By any indirection. I did send
To you for gold to pay my legions.
Which you denied me; was that done like Cassius?
Should I have answered Caius Cassius so?
When Marcus Brutus grows so covetous,
80 To lock such rascal counters from his friends,
Be ready, gods, with all your thunderbolts,
Dash him to pieces!

CASSIUS   I denied you not.

BRUTUS
You did.

CASSIUS   I did not. He was but a fool
That brought my answer back. Brutus hath rived my
          heart;
A friend should bear his friend's infirmities;
But Brutus makes mine greater than they are.

BRUTUS
I do not, till you practise them on me.

CASSIUS
You love me not.

BRUTUS   I do not like your faults.

CASSIUS
A friendly eye could never see such faults.

BRUTUS
90 A flatterer's would not, though they do appear
As huge as high Olympus.

CASSIUS
Come, Antony, and young Octavius, come,
Revenge yourselves alone on Cassius,
For Cassius is aweary of the world;

Hated by one he loves; braved by his brother;
Checked like a bondman; all his faults observed,
Set in a notebook, learned, and conned by rote,
To cast into my teeth. O, I could weep
My spirit from mine eyes! There is my dagger,
And here my naked breast; within, a heart   100
Dearer than Pluto's mine, richer than gold:
If that thou be'st a Roman, take it forth.
I, that denied thee gold, will give my heart:
Strike, as thou didst at Caesar; for I know,
When thou didst hate him worst, thou lovedst him
      better
Than ever thou lovedst Cassius.

BRUTUS   Sheathe your dagger.
Be angry when you will, it shall have scope;
Do what you will, dishonour shall be humour.
O Cassius, you are yokèd with a lamb
That carries anger as the flint bears fire,   110
Who, much enforcèd, shows a hasty spark,
And straight is cold again.

CASSIUS   Hath Cassius lived
To be but mirth and laughter to his Brutus,
When grief and blood ill-tempered vexeth him?

BRUTUS
When I spoke that, I was ill-tempered too.

CASSIUS
Do you confess so much? Give me your hand.

BRUTUS
And my heart too.

CASSIUS   O Brutus!

BRUTUS   What's the matter?

CASSIUS
Have not you love enough to bear with me,
When that rash humour which my mother gave me

123

120 Makes me forgetful?

BRUTUS   Yes, Cassius; and from henceforth,
When you are over-earnest with your Brutus,
He'll think your mother chides, and leave you so.

> *Enter a Poet followed by Lucius; Titinius and Lucilius*
> *attempting to restrain him*

POET
Let me go in to see the Generals.
There is some grudge between 'em; 'tis not meet
They be alone.

LUCILIUS   You shall not come to them.

POET Nothing but death shall stay me.

CASSIUS How now? What's the matter?

POET
For shame, you Generals! What do you mean?
Love, and be friends, as two such men should be;
130 For I have seen more years, I'm sure, than ye.

CASSIUS
Ha, ha! How vilely doth this cynic rhyme!

BRUTUS
Get you hence, sirrah! Saucy fellow, hence!

CASSIUS
Bear with him, Brutus; 'tis his fashion.

BRUTUS
I'll know his humour, when he knows his time.
What should the wars do with these jigging fools?
Companion, hence!

CASSIUS   Away, away, be gone!   *Exit Poet*

BRUTUS
Lucilius and Titinius, bid the commanders
Prepare to lodge their companies tonight.

CASSIUS
And come yourselves, and bring Messala with you
140 Immediately to us.   *Exeunt Lucilius and Titinius*

BRUTUS   Lucius, a bowl of wine. *Exit Lucius*

CASSIUS

I did not think you could have been so angry.

BRUTUS

O Cassius, I am sick of many griefs.

CASSIUS

Of your philosophy you make no use,
If you give place to accidental evils.

BRUTUS

No man bears sorrow better. Portia is dead.

CASSIUS Ha? Portia?

BRUTUS She is dead.

CASSIUS

How 'scaped I killing, when I crossed you so?
O insupportable and touching loss!
Upon what sickness?

BRUTUS   Impatient of my absence,   150
And grief that young Octavius with Mark Antony
Have made themselves so strong; for with her death
That tidings came. With this she fell distract,
And, her attendants absent, swallowed fire.

CASSIUS

And died so?

BRUTUS   Even so.

CASSIUS   O ye immortal gods!
          Enter Boy (Lucius) with wine and tapers

BRUTUS

Speak no more of her. Give me a bowl of wine.
In this I bury all unkindness, Cassius.
          He drinks

CASSIUS

My heart is thirsty for that noble pledge.
Fill, Lucius, till the wine o'erswell the cup;
I cannot drink too much of Brutus' love.   *Exit Lucius* 160

Cassius drinks
Enter Titinius and Messala

BRUTUS

Come in, Titinius. Welcome, good Messala.
Now sit we close about this taper here,
And call in question our necessities.

CASSIUS

Portia, art thou gone?

BRUTUS   No more, I pray you.
Messala, I have here receivèd letters,
That young Octavius and Mark Antony
Come down upon us with a mighty power,
Bending their expedition toward Philippi.

MESSALA

Myself have letters of the self-same tenor.

170 BRUTUS With what addition?

MESSALA

That by proscription and bills of outlawry
Octavius, Antony, and Lepidus
Have put to death an hundred senators.

BRUTUS

Therein our letters do not well agree.
Mine speak of seventy senators that died
By their proscriptions, Cicero being one.

CASSIUS

Cicero one?

MESSALA   Cicero is dead,
And by that order of proscription.
Had you your letters from your wife, my lord?

180 BRUTUS No, Messala.

MESSALA

Nor nothing in your letters writ of her?

BRUTUS

Nothing, Messala.

MESSALA   That, methinks, is strange.
BRUTUS
  Why ask you? Hear you aught of her in yours?
MESSALA No, my lord.
BRUTUS
  Now, as you are a Roman, tell me true.
MESSALA
  Then like a Roman bear the truth I tell;
  For certain she is dead, and by strange manner.
BRUTUS
  Why, farewell, Portia. We must die, Messala.
  With meditating that she must die once,
  I have the patience to endure it now.   190
MESSALA
  Even so great men great losses should endure.
CASSIUS
  I have as much of this in art as you,
  But yet my nature could not bear it so.
BRUTUS
  Well, to our work alive. What do you think
  Of marching to Philippi presently?
CASSIUS
  I do not think it good.
BRUTUS   Your reason?
CASSIUS   This it is:
  'Tis better that the enemy seek us;
  So shall he waste his means, weary his soldiers,
  Doing himself offence, whilst we, lying still,
  Are full of rest, defence, and nimbleness.   200
BRUTUS
  Good reasons must of force give place to better.
  The people 'twixt Philippi and this ground
  Do stand but in a forced affection;
  For they have grudged us contribution.

The enemy, marching along by them,
By them shall make a fuller number up,
Come on refreshed, new-added, and encouraged;
From which advantage shall we cut him off,
If at Philippi we do face him there,
210 These people at our back.

CASSIUS   Hear me, good brother –

BRUTUS

Under your pardon. You must note beside
That we have tried the utmost of our friends,
Our legions are brim-full, our cause is ripe.
The enemy increaseth every day;
We, at the height, are ready to decline.
There is a tide in the affairs of men,
Which, taken at the flood, leads on to fortune;
Omitted, all the voyage of their life
Is bound in shallows and in miseries.
220 On such a full sea are we now afloat,
And we must take the current when it serves,
Or lose our ventures.

CASSIUS   Then, with your will, go on;
We'll along ourselves, and meet them at Philippi.

BRUTUS

The deep of night is crept upon our talk,
And nature must obey necessity,
Which we will niggard with a little rest.
There is no more to say?

CASSIUS   No more. Good night.
Early tomorrow will we rise, and hence.

BRUTUS

Lucius!

    Enter Lucius
       My gown.   *Exit Lucius*
          Farewell, good Messala.

Good night, Titinius. Noble, noble Cassius,   230
Good night, and good repose.

CASSIUS   O my dear brother,
This was an ill beginning of the night;
Never come such division 'tween our souls!
Let it not, Brutus.

    Enter Lucius, with the gown

BRUTUS   Everything is well.

CASSIUS

Good night, my lord.

BRUTUS   Good night, good brother.

TITINIUS *and* MESSALA

Good night, Lord Brutus.

BRUTUS   Farewell, every one.

        Exeunt Cassius, Titinius, and Messala

Give me the gown. Where is thy instrument?

LUCIUS

Here in the tent.

BRUTUS   What, thou speak'st drowsily?
Poor knave, I blame thee not; thou art o'erwatched.
Call Claudius and some other of my men;   240
I'll have them sleep on cushions in my tent.

LUCIUS Varro and Claudius!

    Enter Varro and Claudius

VARRO Calls my lord?

BRUTUS

I pray you, sirs, lie in my tent and sleep;
It may be I shall raise you by and by
On business to my brother Cassius.

VARRO

So please you, we will stand and watch your pleasure.

BRUTUS

I will not have it so; lie down, good sirs.
It may be I shall otherwise bethink me.

Varro and Claudius lie down

250 Look, Lucius, here's the book I sought for so;
I put it in the pocket of my gown.

LUCIUS

I was sure your lordship did not give it me.

BRUTUS

Bear with me, good boy, I am much forgetful.
Canst thou hold up thy heavy eyes awhile,
And touch thy instrument a strain or two?

LUCIUS

Ay, my lord, an't please you.

BRUTUS It does, my boy.
I trouble thee too much, but thou art willing.

LUCIUS It is my duty, sir.

BRUTUS

I should not urge thy duty past thy might;
260 I know young bloods look for a time of rest.

LUCIUS I have slept, my lord, already.

BRUTUS

It was well done, and thou shalt sleep again;
I will not hold thee long. If I do live,
I will be good to thee.

Music, and a song
Lucius falls asleep

This is a sleepy tune; O murderous slumber,
Layest thou thy leaden mace upon my boy,
That plays thee music? Gentle knave, good night;
I will not do thee so much wrong to wake thee.
If thou dost nod, thou break'st thy instrument;
270 I'll take it from thee; and, good boy, good night.
Let me see, let me see; is not the leaf turned down
Where I left reading? Here it is, I think.

He sits and reads
Enter the Ghost of Caesar

How ill this taper burns! Ha! Who comes here?
I think it is the weakness of mine eyes
That shapes this monstrous apparition.
It comes upon me. Art thou any thing?
Art thou some god, some angel, or some devil,
That mak'st my blood cold, and my hair to stare?
Speak to me what thou art.

GHOST

Thy evil spirit, Brutus.

BRUTUS   Why com'st thou?   280

GHOST

To tell thee thou shalt see me at Philippi.

BRUTUS Well; then I shall see thee again?

GHOST Ay, at Philippi.

BRUTUS

Why, I will see thee at Philippi then.   *Exit Ghost*
Now I have taken heart, thou vanishest.
Ill spirit, I would hold more talk with thee.
Boy! Lucius! Varro! Claudius! Sirs, awake!
Claudius!

LUCIUS The strings, my lord, are false.

BRUTUS

He thinks he still is at his instrument.   290
Lucius, awake!

LUCIUS My Lord?

BRUTUS

Didst thou dream, Lucius, that thou so criedst out?

LUCIUS

My lord, I do not know that I did cry.

BRUTUS

Yes, that thou didst. Didst thou see anything?

LUCIUS Nothing, my lord.

BRUTUS

Sleep again, Lucius. Sirrah Claudius!

Fellow thou, awake!

VARRO   My lord?

CLAUDIUS   My lord?

BRUTUS

Why did you so cry out, sirs, in your sleep?

VARRO *and* CLAUDIUS

300   Did we, my lord?

BRUTUS   Ay; saw you anything?

VARRO

No, my lord, I saw nothing.

CLAUDIUS   Nor I, my lord.

BRUTUS

Go, and commend me to my brother Cassius.
Bid him set on his powers betimes before,
And we will follow.

VARRO *and* CLAUDIUS It shall be done, my lord.

Exeunt

*

V.1   *Enter Octavius, Antony, and their army*

OCTAVIUS

Now, Antony, our hopes are answerèd:
You said the enemy would not come down,
But keep the hills and upper regions.
It proves not so; their battles are at hand;
They mean to warn us at Philippi here,
Answering before we do demand of them.

ANTONY

Tut, I am in their bosoms, and I know
Wherefore they do it. They could be content
To visit other places, and come down

132

With fearful bravery, thinking by this face   10
To fasten in our thoughts that they have courage;
But 'tis not so.
> *Enter a Messenger*

MESSENGER   Prepare you, Generals;
The enemy comes on in gallant show.
Their bloody sign of battle is hung out,
And something to be done immediately.

ANTONY
Octavius, lead your battle softly on
Upon the left hand of the even field.

OCTAVIUS
Upon the right hand I. Keep thou the left.

ANTONY
Why do you cross me in this exigent?

OCTAVIUS
I do not cross you; but I will do so.   20
> *March*
> *Drum*
> *Enter Brutus, Cassius, and their army; Lucilius,*
> *Titinius, Messala, and others*

BRUTUS They stand, and would have parley.

CASSIUS
Stand fast, Titinius; we must out and talk.

OCTAVIUS
Mark Antony, shall we give sign of battle?

ANTONY
No, Caesar, we will answer on their charge.
Make forth; the Generals would have some words.

OCTAVIUS Stir not until the signal.

BRUTUS
Words before blows: is it so, countrymen?

OCTAVIUS
Not that we love words better, as you do.

BRUTUS

Good words are better than bad strokes, Octavius.

ANTONY

30 In your bad strokes, Brutus, you give good words;
Witness the hole you made in Caesar's heart,
Crying, 'Long live! Hail, Caesar!'

CASSIUS   Antony,
The posture of your blows are yet unknown;
But for your words, they rob the Hybla bees,
And leave them honeyless.

ANTONY   Not stingless too.

BRUTUS O yes, and soundless too;
For you have stolen their buzzing, Antony,
And very wisely threat before you sting.

ANTONY

Villains! You did not so, when your vile daggers
40 Hacked one another in the sides of Caesar:
You showed your teeth like apes, and fawned like
            hounds,
And bowed like bondmen, kissing Caesar's feet;
Whilst damnèd Casca, like a cur, behind
Struck Caesar on the neck. O you flatterers!

CASSIUS

Flatterers? Now, Brutus, thank yourself:
This tongue had not offended so today,
If Cassius might have ruled.

OCTAVIUS

Come, come, the cause. If arguing make us sweat,
The proof of it will turn to redder drops.
50 Look,
I draw a sword against conspirators.
When think you that the sword goes up again?
Never till Caesar's three and thirty wounds
Be well avenged; or till another Caesar

Have added slaughter to the sword of traitors.

BRUTUS
Caesar, thou canst not die by traitors' hands,
Unless thou bring'st them with thee.

OCTAVIUS   So I hope.
I was not born to die on Brutus' sword.

BRUTUS
O, if thou wert the noblest of thy strain,
Young man, thou couldst not die more honourable.   60

CASSIUS
A peevish schoolboy, worthless of such honour,
Joined with a masquer and a reveller.

ANTONY
Old Cassius, still!

OCTAVIUS   Come, Antony; away!
Defiance, traitors, hurl we in your teeth.
If you dare fight today, come to the field;
If not, when you have stomachs.

                    Exeunt Octavius, Antony, and army

CASSIUS
Why now, blow wind, swell billow, and swim bark!
The storm is up, and all is on the hazard.

BRUTUS
Ho, Lucilius, hark, a word with you.

LUCILIUS   My lord?
          Lucilius stands forth, and talks with Brutus apart

CASSIUS
Messala.

MESSALA What says my General?
          Messala stands forth

CASSIUS   Messala,   70
This is my birthday; as this very day
Was Cassius born. Give me thy hand, Messala:
Be thou my witness that against my will —

As Pompey was – am I compelled to set
Upon one battle all our liberties.
You know that I held Epicurus strong,
And his opinion; now I change my mind,
And partly credit things that do presage.
Coming from Sardis, on our former ensign
80 Two mighty eagles fell, and there they perched,
Gorging and feeding from our soldiers' hands,
Who to Philippi here consorted us.
This morning are they fled away and gone,
And in their steads do ravens, crows, and kites
Fly o'er our heads and downward look on us,
As we were sickly prey; their shadows seem
A canopy most fatal, under which
Our army lies, ready to give up the ghost.

MESSALA

Believe not so.

CASSIUS   I but believe it partly,
90 For I am fresh of spirit, and resolved
To meet all perils very constantly.

BRUTUS

Even so, Lucilius.

      Brutus rejoins Cassius

CASSIUS   Now, most noble Brutus,
The gods today stand friendly, that we may,
Lovers in peace, lead on our days to age!
But since the affairs of men rests still incertain,
Let's reason with the worst that may befall.
If we do lose this battle, then is this
The very last time we shall speak together;
What are you then determinèd to do?

BRUTUS

100 Even by the rule of that philosophy
By which I did blame Cato for the death

Which he did give himself – I know not how,
But I do find it cowardly and vile,
For fear of what might fall, so to prevent
The time of life – arming myself with patience
To stay the providence of some high powers
That govern us below.

CASSIUS   Then, if we lose this battle,
You are contented to be led in triumph
Thorough the streets of Rome?

BRUTUS
No, Cassius, no; think not, thou noble Roman,   110
That ever Brutus will go bound to Rome;
He bears too great a mind. But this same day
Must end that work the ides of March begun;
And whether we shall meet again I know not.
Therefore our everlasting farewell take:
For ever, and for ever, farewell, Cassius.
If we do meet again, why, we shall smile;
If not, why then this parting was well made.

CASSIUS
For ever, and for ever, farewell, Brutus.
If we do meet again, we'll smile indeed;   120
If not, 'tis true this parting was well made.

BRUTUS
Why then, lead on. O, that a man might know
The end of this day's business ere it come!
But it sufficeth that the day will end,
And then the end is known. Come, ho! Away! *Exeunt*

Alarum   V.2
Enter Brutus and Messala

BRUTUS
Ride, ride, Messala, ride, and give these bills

Unto the legions on the other side.
>   *Loud alarum*
Let them set on at once; for I perceive
But cold demeanour in Octavius' wing,
And sudden push gives them the overthrow.
Ride, ride, Messala; let them all come down.

>   *Exeunt*

V.3   *Alarums*
>   *Enter Cassius and Titinius*

CASSIUS

O, look, Titinius, look, the villains fly.
Myself have to mine own turned enemy:
This Ensign here of mine was turning back;
I slew the coward, and did take it from him.

TITINIUS

O Cassius, Brutus gave the word too early,
Who, having some advantage on Octavius,
Took it too eagerly; his soldiers fell to spoil,
Whilst we by Antony are all enclosed.
>   *Enter Pindarus*

PINDARUS

Fly further off, my lord, fly further off!
Mark Antony is in your tents, my lord.
Fly therefore, noble Cassius, fly far off!

CASSIUS

This hill is far enough. Look, look, Titinius!
Are those my tents where I perceive the fire?

TITINIUS

They are, my lord.

CASSIUS   Titinius, if thou lov'st me,
Mount thou my horse, and hide thy spurs in him,
Till he have brought thee up to yonder troops

10

And here again, that I may rest assured
Whether yond troops are friend or enemy.

TITINIUS
I will be here again, even with a thought.   *Exit*

CASSIUS
Go, Pindarus, get higher on that hill;   20
My sight was ever thick. Regard Titinius,
And tell me what thou not'st about the field.
    Pindarus ascends
This day I breathèd first. Time is come round,
And where I did begin, there shall I end.
My life is run his compass. (*To Pindarus*) Sirrah, what
    news?

PINDARUS (*above*) O my lord!

CASSIUS What news?

PINDARUS
Titinius is enclosèd round about
With horsemen, that make to him on the spur,
Yet he spurs on. Now they are almost on him.   30
Now, Titinius! Now some light. O, he lights too!
He's ta'en!
    Shout
        And hark! They shout for joy.

CASSIUS Come down; behold no more.
O, coward that I am, to live so long,
To see my best friend ta'en before my face!
    Enter Pindarus from above
Come hither, sirrah.
In Parthia did I take thee prisoner;
And then I swore thee, saving of thy life,
That whatsoever I did bid thee do,
Thou shouldst attempt it. Come now, keep thine oath;   40
Now be a freeman; and with this good sword,
That ran through Caesar's bowels, search this bosom.

Stand not to answer. Here, take thou the hilts,
And when my face is covered, as 'tis now,
Guide thou the sword. – Caesar, thou art revenged,
Even with the sword that killed thee.   *He dies*

PINDARUS

So, I am free; yet would not so have been,
Durst I have done my will. O Cassius!
Far from this country Pindarus shall run,
50 Where never Roman shall take note of him.   *Exit*
   Enter Titinius and Messala

MESSALA

It is but change, Titinius; for Octavius
Is overthrown by noble Brutus' power,
As Cassius' legions are by Antony.

TITINIUS

These tidings will well comfort Cassius.

MESSALA

Where did you leave him?

TITINIUS   All disconsolate,
With Pindarus his bondman, on this hill.

MESSALA

Is not that he that lies upon the ground?

TITINIUS

He lies not like the living. O my heart!

MESSALA

Is not that he?

TITINIUS   No, this was he, Messala,
60 But Cassius is no more. O setting sun,
As in thy red rays thou dost sink to night,
So in his red blood Cassius' day is set.
The sun of Rome is set. Our day is gone;
Clouds, dews, and dangers come; our deeds are done.
Mistrust of my success hath done this deed.

MESSALA

Mistrust of good success hath done this deed.
O hateful Error, Melancholy's child,
Why dost thou show to the apt thoughts of men
The things that are not? O Error, soon conceived,
Thou never com'st unto a happy birth,   70
But kill'st the mother that engendered thee.

TITINIUS

What, Pindarus! Where art thou, Pindarus?

MESSALA

Seek him, Titinius, whilst I go to meet
The noble Brutus, thrusting this report
Into his ears. I may say 'thrusting' it;
For piercing steel and darts envenomèd
Shall be as welcome to the ears of Brutus
As tidings of this sight.

TITINIUS   Hie you, Messala,
And I will seek for Pindarus the while.   *Exit Messala*
Why didst thou send me forth, brave Cassius?   80
Did I not meet thy friends, and did not they
Put on my brows this wreath of victory,
And bid me give it thee? Didst thou not hear their
      shouts?
Alas, thou hast misconstrued everything!
But hold thee, take this garland on thy brow;
Thy Brutus bid me give it thee, and I
Will do his bidding. Brutus, come apace,
And see how I regarded Caius Cassius.
By your leave, gods. This is a Roman's part;
Come, Cassius' sword, and find Titinius' heart.   90

He dies

Alarum
*Enter Brutus, Messala, Young Cato, Strato, Volum-
nius, Labeo, Flavius, and Lucilius*

141

BRUTUS

Where, where, Messala, doth his body lie?

MESSALA

Lo, yonder, and Titinius mourning it.

BRUTUS

Titinius' face is upward.

CATO   He is slain.

BRUTUS

O Julius Caesar, thou art mighty yet!
Thy spirit walks abroad, and turns our swords
In our own proper entrails.

    Low alarums

CATO   Brave Titinius,

Look where he have not crowned dead Cassius.

BRUTUS

Are yet two Romans living such as these?
The last of all the Romans, fare thee well!
It is impossible that ever Rome
Should breed thy fellow. Friends, I owe more tears
To this dead man than you shall see me pay.
I shall find time, Cassius, I shall find time.
Come therefore, and to Thasos send his body.
His funerals shall not be in our camp,
Lest it discomfort us. Lucilius, come;
And come, young Cato; let us to the field.
Labeo and Flavius, set our battles on.
'Tis three o'clock; and, Romans, yet ere night
We shall try fortune in a second fight.   *Exeunt*

*Enter Brutus, Messala, Young Cato, Lucilius, and
Flavius*

BRUTUS

Yet countrymen, O, yet hold up your heads!
                    Exit, followed by Messala and Flavius

CATO

What bastard doth not? Who will go with me?
I will proclaim my name about the field.
I am the son of Marcus Cato, ho!
A foe to tyrants, and my country's friend.
I am the son of Marcus Cato, ho!
    Enter soldiers, and fight

LUCILIUS

And I am Brutus, Marcus Brutus, I!
Brutus, my country's friend; know me for Brutus!
                              Young Cato is slain

O young and noble Cato, art thou down?
Why, now thou diest as bravely as Titinius,   10
And mayst be honoured, being Cato's son.

FIRST SOLDIER

Yield, or thou diest.

LUCILIUS   Only I yield to die.
There is so much that thou wilt kill me straight:
Kill Brutus, and be honoured in his death.

FIRST SOLDIER We must not. A noble prisoner!
    Enter Antony

SECOND SOLDIER

Room, ho! Tell Antony, Brutus is ta'en.

FIRST SOLDIER

I'll tell the news. Here comes the General.
Brutus is ta'en, Brutus is ta'en, my lord.

ANTONY Where is he?

LUCILIUS

20 Safe, Antony; Brutus is safe enough.
I dare assure thee that no enemy
Shall ever take alive the noble Brutus;
The gods defend him from so great a shame!
When you do find him, or alive or dead,
He will be found like Brutus, like himself.

ANTONY

This is not Brutus, friend; but, I assure you,
A prize no less in worth. Keep this man safe;
Give him all kindness. I had rather have
Such men my friends than enemies. Go on,
30 And see where Brutus be alive or dead;
And bring us word unto Octavius' tent
How every thing is chanced.   *Exeunt*

V.5   *Enter Brutus, Dardanius, Clitus, Strato, and Volumnius*

BRUTUS

Come, poor remains of friends, rest on this rock.

CLITUS

Statilius showed the torch-light; but, my lord,
He came not back; he is or ta'en or slain.

BRUTUS

Sit thee down, Clitus. Slaying is the word;
It is a deed in fashion. Hark thee, Clitus.
        He whispers

CLITUS

What, I, my lord? No, not for all the world.

BRUTUS

' Peace then. No words.

CLITUS   I'll rather kill myself.

BRUTUS

Hark thee, Dardanius.

He whispers

DARDANIUS   Shall I do such a deed?

CLITUS O Dardanius!

DARDANIUS O Clitus!   10

CLITUS

    What ill request did Brutus make to thee?

DARDANIUS

    To kill him, Clitus. Look, he meditates.

CLITUS

    Now is that noble vessel full of grief,

    That it runs over even at his eyes.

BRUTUS

    Come hither, good Volumnius; list a word.

VOLUMNIUS

    What says my lord?

BRUTUS   Why, this, Volumnius:

    The ghost of Caesar hath appeared to me

    Two several times by night: at Sardis once,

    And this last night, here in Philippi fields.

    I know my hour is come.

VOLUMNIUS   Not so, my lord.   20

BRUTUS

    Nay, I am sure it is, Volumnius.

    Thou seest the world, Volumnius, how it goes:

    Our enemies have beat us to the pit.

       Low alarums

    It is more worthy to leap in ourselves

    Than tarry till they push us. Good Volumnius,

    Thou know'st that we two went to school together;

    Even for that our love of old, I prithee

    Hold thou my sword-hilts whilst I run on it.

VOLUMNIUS

    That's not an office for a friend, my lord.

       Alarum still

CLITUS

30 Fly, fly, my lord, there is no tarrying here.

BRUTUS

Farewell to you; and you; and you, Volumnius.
Strato, thou hast been all this while asleep;
Farewell to thee too, Strato. Countrymen,
My heart doth joy that yet in all my life
I found no man but he was true to me.
I shall have glory by this losing day
More than Octavius and Mark Antony
By this vile conquest shall attain unto.
So fare you well at once; for Brutus' tongue
40 Hath almost ended his life's history.
Night hangs upon mine eyes; my bones would rest,
That have but laboured to attain this hour.
Alarum
Cry within, 'Fly, fly, fly!'

CLITUS

Fly, my lord, fly!

BRUTUS   Hence! I will follow.
                    Exeunt Clitus, Dardanius, and Volumnius
I prithee, Strato, stay thou by thy lord.
Thou art a fellow of a good respect;
Thy life hath had some smatch of honour in it.
Hold then my sword, and turn away thy face,
While I do run upon it. Wilt thou, Strato?

STRATO

Give me your hand first. Fare you well, my lord.

BRUTUS

50 Farewell, good Strato. – Caesar, now be still;
I killed not thee with half so good a will.   *He dies*
      Alarum
      Retreat

*Enter Antony, Octavius, Messala, Lucilius, and the
army*

OCTAVIUS What man is that?

MESSALA
  My master's man. Strato, where is thy master?

STRATO
  Free from the bondage you are in, Messala.
  The conquerors can but make a fire of him;
  For Brutus only overcame himself,
  And no man else hath honour by his death.

LUCILIUS
  So Brutus should be found. I thank thee, Brutus,
  That thou hast proved Lucilius' saying true.

OCTAVIUS
  All that served Brutus, I will entertain them.   60
  Fellow, wilt thou bestow thy time with me?

STRATO
  Ay, if Messala will prefer me to you.

OCTAVIUS Do so, good Messala.

MESSALA How died my master, Strato?

STRATO
  I held the sword, and he did run on it.

MESSALA
  Octavius, then take him to follow thee,
  That did the latest service to my master.

ANTONY
  This was the noblest Roman of them all.
  All the conspirators save only he
  Did that they did in envy of great Caesar;   70
  He only, in a general honest thought
  And common good to all, made one of them.
  His life was gentle, and the elements
  So mixed in him, that Nature might stand up
  And say to all the world, 'This was a man!'

147

OCTAVIUS

    According to his virtue let us use him,
    With all respect and rites of burial.
    Within my tent his bones tonight shall lie,
    Most like a soldier, ordered honourably.
80 So call the field to rest, and let's away,
    To part the glories of this happy day.   *Exeunt all*

COMMENTARY

The act and scene divisions are those of Peter Alexander's edition of the *Complete Works*, London, 1951. All references to other plays by Shakespeare are to this edition. References to North's Plutarch are to *Shakespeare's Plutarch* edited by T. J. B. Spencer (Penguin Books, 1964).

The Characters in the Play

There is a good deal of inconsistency in the form of some of these names in the Folio text, and many of them differ from both the Roman forms and those used by North. For example, the Folio has *Murellus* or *Murrellus*, *Antonio*, *Flavio*, *Labio*, *Octavio*, *Varrus*, and *Claudio*. Most previous editors of the play have changed these so that they conform to North's usage. However, they have also inconsistently retained the Folio's *Portia*, *Lena*, and *Dardanius* rather than replaced them with North's *Porcia*, *Laena*, and *Dardanus*. Although editorial consistency is desirable, it is probably impractical in this case, owing to the number of reference and critical works keyed to the practice of earlier editions. I have, therefore, followed the well-established 'tradition' of inconsistency.

Both *Calphurnia* and *Calpurnia* are used by North, and many previous editors have favoured the latter form. As the Folio is consistent in its use of the former, I have retained it in this text.

There are two characters, Labeo and Flavius, who appear in V.3 and 4 but do not speak.

I.1   (stage direction) *Flavius, Marullus*. In Plutarch these are Tribunes of the People; but Shakespeare makes them also partisans of Pompey, which is their main function in this scene, so that they may display an antagonism to

149

Caesar and his ambitions which prepares the audience for the later enmity of Brutus and Cassius.

over the stage. This is probably an indication for the crowd to enter first and swarm about the stage prior to the entrance of the Tribunes.

3   *Being mechanical* belonging to the artisan class

4–5   *without the sign | Of your profession.* No particular sign is referred to here; Flavius merely means 'not having tools and not wearing working clothes'; see lines 7–8.

10   *in respect of* in comparison with

11   *cobbler.* The pun is on (1) 'shoe-mender', (2) 'bungler', 'botcher'. This character is probably derived from Plutarch's phrase 'cobblers, tapsters, or suchlike base mechanical people' (*Brutus*, pages 112–13).

12   *directly* straightforwardly, without quibbling

14   *soles.* The pun is on (1) 'bottoms of shoes', (2) 'souls'.

15   *What trade, thou knave? Thou naughty knave, what trade?* Many editors give this speech to Marullus on the grounds that Flavius is the more conciliatory of the two. Shakespeare is obviously distributing the speeches to keep both actors occupied; and the cobbler finds no difficulty in speaking to both in the following lines.

        naughty worthless, rascally

16   *be not out with me* do not be angry with me. The pun is with 'out' in line 17 meaning 'out at heels, with worn shoes'.

17   *mend.* The pun is on (1) 'repair' (shoes), (2) 'reform' (souls).

19   *cobble you* mend your shoes. This makes clear to Marullus the cobbler's trade which is still in doubt for him owing to the punning in lines 10–17.

21–3   *Truly, sir . . . old shoes.* The cobbler continues his punning with the play on 'awl' and 'all', and also on 'meddle' meaning 'to interfere' and 'to have sexual relations'. This passage may contain an allusion to Thomas Dekker's play, *The Shoemakers' Holiday*, which was acted in 1599, and in which the hero, Simon Eyre, claims not to interfere with concerns which lie outside the practice of his trade as cobbler.

24   *recover*. The pun is on (1) 're-sole', 'patch', (2) 'restore to health'.

24–5   *As proper men as ever trod upon neat's leather* (a proverbial expression meaning 'as handsome men as ever walked in shoes made of cowhide')

31   *triumph*. This was a procession celebrating a military victory. Caesar defeated Cnaeus and Sextus, the sons of Pompey the Great, at Munda in Spain on 17 March 45 B.C.; and his triumph took place at the beginning of October the same year.

32–4   *Wherefore rejoice? . . . wheels?* Shakespeare based these lines on a passage in Plutarch's *Caesar*:

> *But the Triumph he made into Rome . . . did as much offend the Romans, and more, than anything that ever he had done before; because he had not overcome captains that were strangers, nor barbarous kings, but had destroyed the sons of the noblest man in Rome, whom fortune had overthrown. And, because he had plucked up his race by the roots, men did not think it meet for him to triumph so for the calamities of his country* (pages 76–7).

33   *tributaries* captives who will pay tribute

34   *grace* pay honour to
       captive bonds fetters

35   *senseless* without feelings

37   *Pompey* (Pompey the Great, defeated by Caesar in 48 B.C., and later assassinated)

42   *pass the streets* pass through the streets

46   *replication* reverberation

47   *concave shores* hollowed-out or overhanging banks (which create an echo)

49   *cull out a holiday* pick out a working-day and turn it into a holiday. The verb was probably suggested by association with 'flowers' in line 50; which idea

Shakespeare took from Plutarch's remark 'there were some that cast flowers ... as they commonly use to do unto any man when he hath obtained victory' (*Caesar*, page 52).

51   *Pompey's blood*. The term is used with the double meaning (1) 'Pompey's sons', (2) 'the spilt blood of Pompey in his sons'.

54   *intermit* withhold, suspend. Marullus indicates that a plague is almost the inevitable punishment for the citizens' actions.

59-60   *till the lowest stream ... of all* so that the river level even at its lowest ebb may rise to the highest banks

61   *where* whether
       mettle temperament, disposition

64-5   *Disrobe the images,* | *If you do find them decked with ceremonies*. Plutarch notes in *Brutus*:

> *Caesar's flatterers ... beside many other exceeding and unspeakable honours they daily devised for him, in the night-time they did put diadems upon the heads of his images, supposing thereby to allure the common people to call him King, instead of Dictator* (page 110).

65   *ceremonies* symbols of rule

67   *the feast of Lupercal*. This feast of expiation and purification was held in honour of Lupercus, the god of shepherds, on 15 February. Shakespeare combines this with the day of Caesar's triumph (see note to line 31) for dramatic effect; the two events are dealt with separately by Plutarch.

68-71   *let no images ... thick*. This is based on Plutarch's *Caesar*: 'Those [diadems] the two Tribunes, Flavius and Marullus, went and pulled down; and furthermore, meeting with them that first saluted Caesar as king, they committed them to prison' (page 83).

68   *images* statues

69   *trophies* ornaments (such as the 'scarfs' mentioned by

Casca at I.2.282, or the 'diadems' and laurel crown of
Plutarch's account)
about go about

70   *the vulgar* the common people

72–3   *These growing feathers plucked from Caesar's wing | Will*
make him fly an ordinary pitch. The metaphor here is
from falconry: Flavius sees their actions as stripping
Caesar of some of his power, even as a falcon with
plucked wings would have a lower 'pitch', which is the
height soared to before diving.

74   *above the view of men* beyond human sight. This is the
first of many references to Caesar as superman, many
of them, as here, coming from his enemies; compare
I.2.60, 115–16.

I.2   (stage direction) *Antony, stripped for the course.* Plutarch
in his *Caesar* describes the 'holy chase' thus:

> *that day there are divers noblemen's sons, young men ...*
> *which run naked through the city, striking in sport them*
> *they meet in their way with leather thongs, hair and all*
> *on, to make them give place. . . . Antonius, who was*
> *Consul at that time, was one of them that ran this holy*
> *course* (pages 82–3).

6–9   *Forget not ... curse.* Plutarch makes no mention of
Calphurnia's sterility; but states the general Roman
belief:

> *And many noblewomen and gentlewomen also go of pur-*
> *pose to stand in their way, and do put forth their hands*
> *to be stricken, . . . persuading themselves that, being*
> *with child, they shall have good delivery, and also, being*
> *barren, that it will make them to conceive with child*
> (*Caesar*, page 82).

11   *Set on* proceed

15   *press* crowd

17   *Caesar is turned to hear.* Caesar's use of the third person here indicates his arrogance, and reflects his practice in his writings. If line 212 indicates that Caesar is deaf (see note) then the phrase here may be taken literally.

18   *Beware the ides of March.* This is based on Plutarch's *Caesar*: 'there was a certain soothsayer that had given Caesar warning long time afore, to take heed of the day of the Ides of March ... for on that day he should be in great danger' (pages 87–8). The 'ides' means the half-way point in the month; in March, the 15th.

19   *A soothsayer bids you beware the ides of March.* The repetition is dramatically effective in fixing the remark in the audience's mind; but it is also ironical in that it is Brutus's first utterance in the play.

24   *Pass* advance
     (stage direction) *Sennet* (a flourish of trumpets indicating a ceremonial exit)

25   *the order of the course* the progress of the race

28–9 *I am not gamesome: I do lack some part | Of that quick spirit that is in Antony.* Brutus is probably hinting, by quibbles, at his disapproval of the scene he has just witnessed; with 'gamesome' meaning (1) 'sport-loving', (2) 'frivolous'; and 'quick' meaning (1) 'speedy in running', (2) 'lively in disposition', (3) 'prompt (to comply with Caesar's whims)'.

33–4 *I have not from your eyes that gentleness | And show of love as I was wont to have.* Shakespeare changes his source here in making Brutus's worries about Caesar's ambitions the reason for his coldness to Cassius. In Plutarch the hostility between them developed by virtue of Caesar's granting Brutus a praetorship for which Cassius was a rival candidate, an action which was also 'the first cause of Cassius' malice against Caesar'.

33   *gentleness* well-bred courtesy

34   *show* manifestation
     wont accustomed

35   *too strange a hand*. The metaphor is from horsemanship.
strange hostile

37-9 *if I have veiled my look, | I turn the trouble of my coun-
tenance | Merely upon myself* if my face has worn a
troubled look, the expression has been directed only
toward myself not to the beholder of it. Portia makes
the same point about Brutus's recent behaviour at
II.1.242.

39   *Merely* entirely, solely

40   *passions of some difference* conflicting emotions. This is
the crux of Brutus's dilemma: the tension between his
affection for Caesar and his own political ideals. See
also line 46.

41   *Conceptions only proper to myself* thoughts pertaining
only to me

42   *soil* blemish, taint

45   *Nor construe any further my neglect* do not make anything more of my neglect of you. The accent is on the
first syllable in 'construe'.

48   *passion* feelings

50   *worthy* important

54   *just* true

55-62 *And it is very much . . . his eyes*. This is based on
Plutarch's account in *Brutus*:

> *Cassius being bold, and taking hold of this word, 'Why,'
> quoth he, 'what Roman is he alive that will suffer thee
> to die for the liberty? What, knowest thou not that thou
> art Brutus? . . . The noblest men and best citizens . . .
> specially require, as a due debt unto them, the taking
> away of the tyranny, being fully bent to suffer any
> extremity for thy sake, so that thou wilt show thyself to
> be the man thou art taken for, and that they hope thou
> art'* (pages 112-13).

56   *turn* reflect

58   *shadow* image

59   *of the best respect* of the people held in highest estimation

60   *immortal Caesar.* Cassius's first reference to Caesar is highly sarcastic, but ironically it is from him that we receive the most colourfully, and therefore most memorably, phrased evidence of how Caesar was viewed by the majority of Romans; compare lines 134–7.

62   *had his eyes.* There are two possible meanings here: (1) 'were using his eyes properly' (to see Caesar's tyranny), (2) 'had the speaker's eyes' (saw Caesar as the speaker did).

66   *Therefore.* This may mean 'so far as that is concerned', or, as many editors have suggested, that Cassius is merely side-stepping Brutus's doubts in order to proceed with his own line of thought.

68   *glass* mirror

69   *modestly discover* make known without exaggeration

71   *jealous on* suspicious of

72   *laughter.* The Folio reading has been retained with the meaning 'an object of laughter'; compare Brutus's lines at IV.3.49. The two most common emendations are 'laugher' meaning 'jester', and 'loffer' meaning 'lover'.

73–4   *To stale with ordinary oaths my love | To every new protester* to make stale, or cheapen, my affection to every new acquaintance who makes a declaration of friendship for me, by using commonplace oaths. There is perhaps the sense of 'tavern oaths' in the use of 'ordinary'.

76   *after scandal them* later libel them

77   *profess myself* declare friendship

78   *all the rout* the whole common rabble

       (stage direction) *Flourish and shout.* The noises off stage in this scene are used by Shakespeare to keep the audience in mind of the presence of Caesar and the Roman people. Notice his use here of the close juxtaposition of Cassius's despising reference to the crowd and the behaviour of the people to whom Caesar is at this moment pandering.

85-9 *If it be . . . death.* This is a much discussed passage of which several explanations have been given. The difficulty is caused chiefly by (1) whether 'indifferently' means 'with indifference' or 'impartially', and (2) what Brutus means by 'honour'. I take the meaning to be: 'In matters concerning the public welfare, my honour demands that if death is the alternative to its exercise then I will die. For let the fates make me prosper only in proportion to the degree to which I put my honour above my personal safety.' The relevant passage in Plutarch's *Brutus* is: ' "For myself then," said Brutus, "I mean not to hold my peace, but to withstand it, and rather die than lose my liberty." ' (page 112)

91 *outward favour* external features

92 *Well, honour is the subject of my story.* Cassius seizes upon Brutus's use of the word 'honour' and takes it to mean 'reputation', 'status in the city'.

95-6 *I had as lief not be as live to be | In awe of such a thing as I myself.* This and the following lines are based on Plutarch's hint: 'Cassius being a choleric man and hating Caesar privately, more than he did the tyranny openly, he incensed Brutus against him' (*Brutus*, page 109).

95 *I had as lief not be* I would just as soon be dead. There is the possibility of a quibble on 'lief' and 'life'.

99-128 *Endure the winter's . . . sick girl.* Plutarch gives the opposite impression of Caesar:

> . . . yet therefore [he] yielded not to the disease of his body, to make it a cloak to cherish him withal, but, contrarily, took the pains of war as a medicine to cure his sick body, fighting always with his disease, travelling continually, living soberly, and commonly lying abroad in the field (*Caesar*, page 37).

100–15 *For once, upon a raw and gusty day . . . Caesar.* This swimming match and its outcome is Shakespeare's own invention; both Plutarch and Suetonius, in his Life of Caesar included in his book, *Lives of the Twelve Caesars*, make special mention of Caesar's prowess as a swimmer.

101 *chafing with her shores* resenting the constraint constituted by the banks of the river

109 *hearts of controversy* hearts eager for competition with the waves and with each other

112–14 *as Aeneas, our great ancestor,* | *Did from the flames of Troy upon his shoulder* | *The old Anchises bear.* According to Virgil's *Aeneid*, II. 721 ff., Aeneas was the progenitor of the Roman nation who rescued his father, Anchises, from the city of Troy after it had been burned by the Greeks.

117 *bend his body* make an obeisance

119–24 *He had a fever . . . groan.* This is based on Plutarch's account of Caesar's health: 'he was lean, white, and soft skinned, and often subject to headache, and otherwhile to the falling sickness (the which took him the first time, as it is reported, in Corduba, a city of Spain)' (*Caesar*, page 37).

122 *His coward lips did from their colour fly.* Shakespeare evokes the comparison of a soldier deserting his flag, to vivify the simple evidence of cowardice.

123 *bend* direction, inclination (of a look or glance)

124 *his* its

125–6 *Ay, and that tongue of his, that bade the Romans* | *Mark him and write his speeches in their books.* Shakespeare here makes specific the general remark of Plutarch's *Caesar*:

> *It is reported that Caesar had an excellent natural gift to speak well before the people; and, besides that rare gift, he was excellently well studied, so that doubtless he was counted the second man for eloquence in his time* (page 23).

126   *books* writing tablets

127   '*Alas!*' It is possible that this is not part of Caesar's reported words, but Cassius being sarcastic.

        Titinius. According to Plutarch he was 'one of Cassius's chiefest friends', for which see IV.2 and V.3.

128   *amaze* stupefy

129   *temper* temperament, disposition, constitution

130   *get the start of* (a metaphor from racing: 'outstrip and carry off the prize' – 'bear the palm')

131   (stage direction) *Shout. Flourish.* Just as the first off-stage noise at line 78 was timed to appear in conjunction with Cassius's remarks about the 'rout', and thus stimulate Brutus's fears about Caesar's power over the mob, so here the stage direction is associated with the crowning of Caesar.

135   *Colossus.* Shakespeare probably had in mind the most famous giant statue of antiquity: the hundred-foot image of Apollo at Rhodes, which was one of the seven wonders of the world, and in some accounts was said to straddle the harbour.

137   *dishonourable graves* (the graves of bondmen)

138   *Men at some time are masters of their fates.* Brutus echoes this sentiment at IV.3.217–20.

139   *our stars.* The reference is to the basic astrological belief that a man's character and behaviour are governed by the relative positions of the planets at the time of his birth.

142   *be sounded more* resound more famously

145   *conjure with 'em* conjure (up spirits) with them

146   *start* raise up

150   *the breed* the art of breeding

        bloods. The quibble is on (1) 'stock', (2) 'disposition', 'spirit', 'temper'. Cassius may purposely be alluding here to Brutus's lineage of which he is so conscious.

151   *great flood.* The reference is to the inundation of the earth by Zeus, when only Deucalion, King of Phthia, and his wife, Pyrrha, were saved.

152   *famed with* celebrated for

154   *walls*. The verb 'encompassed' demands the emenda-
       tion. While the adjective 'wide' appears to justify the
       Folio reading 'walkes', it can also mean 'extensive, ex-
       tending over a large space or region'.

155   *Rome indeed, and room enough.* This is a pun, as the
       words were apparently pronounced identically in Eliza-
       bethan English.

158   *a Brutus once.* Compare:

       > Marcus Brutus came of that Junius Brutus for whom
       > the ancient Romans made his statue of brass to be set up
       > in the Capitol with the images of the kings, holding a
       > naked sword in his hand, because he had valiantly put
       > down the Tarquins from their kingdom of Rome
       > (Plutarch's *Brutus*, page 102).

       brooked tolerated

159   *eternal* (here used to express extreme abhorrence, prob-
       ably by confusion with 'infernal'; or perhaps the con-
       notation is 'eternally damned')
       to keep his state to maintain his court

161–9 *That you . . . things.* This is Brutus's characteristic
       mode of speech, composed of balanced and antithetical
       phrases, the best example of which is his funeral oration
       in III.2. The whole speech is really an answer to
       Cassius at line 71; he almost ignores Cassius's personal
       animosity toward Caesar.

161   *nothing jealous* not at all uncertain

162   *work* persuade
       aim guess, conjecture, idea

164   *present* moment

165   *so with love I might entreat you* if I may ask you as a
       friend

166   *moved* urged

169   *meet* suitable, fitting
       high things important affairs

170 *chew upon* ponder, consider

173 *these* such

178 *pluck Casca by the sleeve*. This is an anachronism; togas had no sleeves.

180 *worthy note* worthy of notice

185 *ferret* fiery, blood-shot (with anger or resentment)

187 *conference* debate, argument

191-4 *Let me have . . . dangerous*. Shakespeare here conflates two incidents given by Plutarch:

> *Caesar also had Cassius in great jealousy and suspected him much. Whereupon he said on a time to his friends: 'What will Cassius do, think ye? I like not his pale looks.' Another time, when Caesar's friends complained unto him of Antonius and Dolabella, that they pretended some mischief towards him, he answered them again: 'As for those fat men and smooth-combed heads,' quoth he, 'I never reckon of them. But these pale-visaged and carrion lean people, I fear them most' – meaning Brutus and Cassius (Caesar, page 85; see also Brutus, page 109).*

196 *well given* well-disposed. Shakespeare takes the phrase from Plutarch, who notes that Cassius was 'Brutus' familiar friend, but not so well given and conditioned as he'.

198 *my name*. This is a periphrasis typical of the arrogance of both the public and the private Caesar.

201-2 *he looks | Quite through the deeds of men* he looks behind men's actions to determine their motives

202-3 *He loves no plays, | As thou dost, Antony*. According to Plutarch, Antony 'himself passed away the time in hearing of foolish plays' (*Antonius*, page 183); for a full account of Antony's proclivity for revelling, see the same passage.

203 *he hears no music*. There lies behind this idea the Platonic belief that the man in whose nature the elements

are harmoniously blended loves music naturally; on the contrary

> *The man that hath no music in himself,*
> *Nor is not moved with concord of sweet sounds,*
> *Is fit for treasons, stratagems, and spoils ; . . .*
> *Let no such man be trusted.*
>
> (*The Merchant of Venice*, V.1.83–5, 88)

204 *sort* way, manner

210–11 *I rather tell thee what is to be feared | Than what I fear ;*
for always I am Caesar. Plutarch in his *Caesar* gave
Shakespeare the hint for this when he relates how
Cornelius Balbus prevented Caesar from rising before
the Senate: 'What, do you not remember that you are
Caesar, and will you not let them reverence you and do
their duties?' (page 82).

212–13 *Come on my right hand, for this ear is deaf, | And tell me*
truly what thou think'st of him. There is no foundation
for Caesar's deafness in Plutarch; and these lines have
been used as evidence of Shakespeare's stressing Caesar's
physical defects, and of his juxtaposing them with
arrogant claims to semi-divinity. However, it has been
pointed out that Shakespeare may here be using merely
a common proverbial expression which is explained by
a contemporary as 'It is the same that we use to speak
proverbially, when we hear a thing that liketh us not,
saying thus "I cannot hear in that side".'

216 *sad* serious, grave. The phrase is derived from Plutarch's
account of Caesar's return to Rome from Alba: 'he
went his way heavy and sorrowful' (*Caesar*, page 81).

219 *there was a crown offered him.* Plutarch gives two accounts of Antony's offering Caesar the crown in his
Caesar (page 83) and in *Antonius* (pages 186–7); it is the
latter that Shakespeare follows the more closely in
Casca's narration in this scene.

220 *put it by* pushed it aside

227   *marry* indeed (originally an oath meaning 'by the Virgin Mary')

228   *gentler than other* less violently than on the previous occasion (hence more reluctantly)

236   *coronets*. This is Shakespeare's Tudor version of the symbolic 'laurel crown ... having a royal band or diadem wreathed about it' of Plutarch.

237   *fain* willingly

241   *still* each time

241-2 *the rabblement hooted, and clapped their chopped hands.* Shakespeare brings together details from Plutarch's two accounts: 'But when Caesar refused it again the second time ... all the whole people shouted' (*Caesar*, page 83); and 'as oft also as Caesar refused it, all the people together clapped their hands' (*Antonius*, page 187).

242   *hooted*. There is no need for the emendation 'shouted', as the word is in keeping with the rest of Casca's description of the mob, showing his contempt for their behaviour.

       chopped roughened by manual labour

246   *swooned* fainted. Shakespeare based this incident on Plutarch's account of Caesar's return from Alba in *Caesar*:

> *it is reported that afterwards ... he imputed it to his disease, saying that their wits are not perfect which have his disease of the falling evil, when standing on their feet they speak to the common people, but are soon troubled with a trembling of their body and a sudden dimness and giddiness* (page 81).

249   *soft* slowly

252   *like; he.* The Folio text has no stop between these two words, and consequently implies that Brutus is uncertain that Caesar is epileptic. This is untenable in view of the fact that the two men were close friends,

and that Caesar's illness was common knowledge in Rome.

like likely

253-4 *No, Caesar hath it not; but you, and I,* | *And honest Casca, we have the falling sickness.* Cassius deliberately misunderstands Brutus's term, and takes it to mean that they have fallen under Caesar's sway – that is, that they are bondmen.

256 *the tag-rag people* the rabble

262-4 *he plucked me ope his doublet, and offered them his throat to cut.* After Caesar had offended the senate, Plutarch reports that 'Caesar ... departed home to his house, and tearing open his doublet collar, making his neck bare, he cried aloud to his friends that his throat was ready to offer to any man that would come and cut it' (*Caesar*, page 81).

263 *plucked me ope* opened

doublet a short jacket. The anachronism comes from North's Elizabethan rendering of Amyot's French word '*robe*'.

264 *An* if

a man of any occupation. This could mean either (1) 'a tradesman' (to whom the offer was made), or (2) 'a man of action'.

266-9 *When he came to himself again, he said, if he had done or said anything amiss, he desired their worships to think it was his infirmity.* See note to line 246.

271-2 *Caesar had stabbed their mothers.* A bawdy joke is probably intended here.

278 *an* if

280-81 *it was Greek to me* I could not understand it. However, Plutarch notes in his account of Caesar's murder that Casca, after striking the first blow, cried out 'in Greek to his brother: "Brother, help me"' (*Caesar*, page 93).

281-3 *I could tell you more news too: Marullus and Flavius, for pulling scarfs off Caesar's images, are put to silence.* See

I.1.63–9. In Plutarch the laurel crown offered by Antony 'was afterwards put upon the head of one of Caesar's statues or images, the which one of the Tribunes plucked off.... Howbeit Caesar did turn them out of their offices for it' (*Antonius*, page 187; see also *Caesar*, pages 83–4).

286   *am promised forth* have promised to dine elsewhere

287   *dine* lunch

288   *hold* does not change

292   *blunt* abrupt, unpolished in manner

293   *quick mettle* of lively disposition

294–5   *So is he now in execution | Of any bold or noble enterprise.* Cassius deliberately mistakes Brutus's meaning (as at lines 253–4), and takes 'mettle' to mean 'courage'.

296   *However* in spite of the fact that

      tardy form pretence of slow-wittedness, affectation of dullness

297   *rudeness* rough manner

      good wit intelligence. Cassius's images grow naturally out of the lunch invitation he has just issued to Casca.

298   *disgest* digest

304   *world* the present state of affairs

305–17   *Well, Brutus . . . glancèd at.* This soliloquy illustrates well the difference between Brutus and Cassius. While the former is concerned primarily with the abstract principles of protecting Rome from possible tyranny, the latter is chiefly occupied with making the assassination of Caesar a reality. Thus Cassius can view their duologue with a detachment impossible for the uncalculating and personally involved Brutus.

306   *honourable mettle* upstanding spirit

306–7   *wrought | From that it is disposed* twisted out of its natural inclination. The metaphor comes from alchemy and is based on the 'mettle/metal' quibble. 'Noble' metals (like gold) could not be 'wrought'.

307   *meet* fitting

310   *bear me hard* feel ill-will toward me

311-12   *If I were Brutus now, and he were Cassius, | He should not humour me.* It has been suggested that 'he' in line 312 refers to Caesar rather than Brutus; and that Cassius is expressing the fear that Brutus has been corrupted by Caesar's favour. However, this makes the lines unnecessarily complicated. They obviously mean 'if I were Brutus and he were I, he would not be able to influence me as I have just been moulding him'. See Introduction, page 24.

313   *In several hands* in different kinds of handwriting

315   *tending to the great opinion* concerning the great respect

317   *glancèd at* alluded to

318   *seat him sure* make his position secure

319   *worse days endure* have to put up with even greater tyranny in the future

I.3.3   *all the sway of earth.* There is no agreement about the exact meaning of this phrase; the general sense would appear to be 'the whole earthly realm'.

6   *rived* split

8   *exalted with* raised up to

12   *saucy with* insolent to

14   *anything more wonderful.* This may be intended either seriously or sarcastically; that is, 'anything further that inspired awe', or 'anything that was more awe-inspiring than the things you mention'. Considering Cicero's detached attitude, the latter seems the more probable.

15-28   *A common slave ... shrieking.* This is based on Plutarch's *Caesar*:

> *For, touching the fires in the element and spirits running up and down in the night, and also the solitary birds to be seen at noondays sitting in the great market-place – are not all these signs perhaps worth the noting, in such a wonderful chance as happened? But Strabo the Philosopher writeth that divers men were seen going up*

COMMENTARY I.3

*and down in fire; and, furthermore, that there was a
slave of the soldiers that did cast a marvellous burning
flame out of his hand, insomuch as they that saw it
thought he had been burnt, but, when the fire was out, it
was found he had no hurt* (pages 86–7).

Shakespeare's additions are the shrieking women, and
the lion, which may have been suggested by Plutarch's
account of the escape of the Megarian lions which were
a point of difference between Caesar and Cassius; see
Brutus, page 109.

18   *Not sensible of fire* not feeling the pain of the fire
20   *Against* near to
21   *glazed*. Neither of the emendations suggested ('glared'
     or 'gazed') is necessary; there are many contemporary
     examples of this word being used to mean 'stared',
     'gazed fixedly'.
22   *annoying* harming
22–3 *drawn | Upon a heap* huddled together
26   *bird of night* (the screech-owl, which was considered a
     bird of ill-luck)
29   *conjointly meet* happen together
31   *portentous* ominous
32   *climate* area, region
33   *strange-disposèd* abnormally upset
34   *construe things after their fashion* interpret things in
     their own way. 'Construe' has the stress on the first
     syllable.
35   *Clean from the purpose of the things themselves* quite
     differently from their real import
48   *unbracèd*. This is an anachronism meaning 'with doub-
     let open'.
49   *thunder-stone* thunderbolt
50   *cross* forked
52   *Even in the aim* at the very spot at which it was aimed
53   *tempt* make trial of (by defiance)
54   *part* proper action
56   *astonish* dismay

167

57   *dull* obtuse. Cassius, in his desire to shake Casca out of
his terror, contradicts his own judgement at I.2.294–9.

58   *want* lack

60   *put on* manifest
in wonder in a state of astonishment

64   *Why birds and beasts from quality and kind.* Some editors
have suggested that there is an hiatus in the text at this
point; but allowing for Cassius's excited state, the
meaning is clear enough: 'Why birds and animals seem
to act contrary to their very natures.'

65   *Why old men, fools, and children.* This line has been
explained in two ways: (1) according to proverb lore
these three classes of people have the power of prophecy, (2) that there are so many portents that fools,
dotards, and children are able to interpret them. In
view of the context, the latter is the more plausible.
fools 'naturals' or born idiots
calculate prophesy (originally by astrological or mathe-
matical calculation)

66   *ordinance* usual behaviour as ordained by nature

67   *pre-formèd faculties* naturally endowed characteristics

68   *monstrous* unnatural

71   *state* state of affairs

75   *lion in the Capitol.* Perhaps a reference to the lion in
line 20; but it has been suggested that Shakespeare
may have had in mind the lions of the royal menagerie
which were kept in the Tower and were one of the
sights of Elizabethan London.

77   *prodigious* supernatural, threatening

78   *fearful* dreadful, causing terror
eruptions unnatural happenings

81   *thews* sinews

82   *woe the while!* alas for these days!

84   *Our yoke and sufferance* our submission to tyranny and
our patient acceptance of it

85–8 *Indeed . . . in Italy.* This is an echo of Plutarch's mention of the reason given to Caesar by Decius Brutus

why he should go to the Capitol: that the Senate intended 'to proclaim him king of all the provinces of the Empire of Rome out of Italy, and that he should wear his diadem in all other places both by sea and land' (*Caesar*, page 90).

89–90 *I know where I will wear this dagger then:* | *Cassius from bondage will deliver Cassius.* This may well be a sincere sentiment based on Plutarch's remark that 'Cassius even from his cradle could not abide any manner of tyrants' (*Brutus*, pages 109–10); but see note to I.2.95–6.

91 *Therein* (in the ability to commit suicide)

95 *Can be retentive to the strength of spirit* can imprison the resolute spirit

98 *know all the world besides* let everyone else know

102 *cancel.* This is a legal term meaning 'to annul by legal agreement or bond' and was probably suggested by the legal flavour of 'bondmen'.

106 *he were* he would be
hinds. Two meanings are implied: (1) 'deer', (2) 'servants', 'lowly born'.

108 *trash* twigs, splinters, hedge–cuttings

109 *rubbish* litter (such as results from the decay or repair of buildings)
offal wood chips

111 *vile* valueless

114 *My answer must be made* I shall be called to account for my speech

115 *indifferent* a matter of indifference

117 *fleering* gibing, sneering
my hand let us shake hands on it

118 *Be factious* form a party
griefs grievances

120 *who* whoever

123 *undergo* undertake

125 *by this* by this time
stay wait

126   *Pompey's Porch.* In Plutarch this porch of the theatre erected by Pompey in 55 B.C. is the scene of Caesar's assassination; see *Brutus*, pages 119–20.

128   *complexion of the element* the visible aspect of the skies. Both of these terms are alchemical in origin.

129   *In favour's like* in appearance is like. The Folio text reading cannot be defended; for other emendations see An Account of the Text, page 248.

131   *Stand close* remain concealed

132   *Cinna.* 'One of the traitors to Caesar was also called Cinna' . . . 'who in an oration he made had spoken very evil of Caesar' (Plutarch's *Caesar*, page 98, and *Brutus*, pages 129–30).

134   *find out* look for
       Metellus Cimber. Shakespeare follows Plutarch's nomenclature in *Caesar*; in *Brutus* Plutarch calls him Tullius Cimber. Historically his name was L. Tillius Cimber and he was a close friend of Caesar's before joining the conspirators.

135–6 *incorporate | To* in league with

137   *I am glad on't.* This is a response to Cassius's words about Casca's joining the conspiracy.

142   *Be you content* set your mind at rest

142–6 *Good Cinna . . . statue.* This is based on Plutarch's *Brutus*:

> *his friends . . . by many bills also, did openly call and procure him to do that he did. For, under the image of his ancestor Junius Brutus, that drave the kings out of Rome, they wrote: 'Oh that it pleased the gods thou wert now alive, Brutus.' And again: 'That thou wert here among us now.' His tribunal, or chair, where he gave audience during the time he was Praetor, was full of such bills: 'Brutus, thou art asleep, and art not Brutus indeed'* (page 110).

In his *Caesar* Plutarch notes that these papers were planted 'in the night'.

143   *praetor's chair* (the chair of the chief Roman magistrate; see note to II.4.35)

144   *Where Brutus may but find it* where Brutus alone may find it

145–6   *set this up with wax | Upon old Brutus' statue.* The practice of affixing scrolls to statues was an Elizabethan one. See note to lines 142–6.

148   *Decius Brutus.* His real name was Decimus. Shakespeare uses North's form of the name.

151   *bestow* distribute

152   *repair* return

156   *yields him ours* joins our faction

159   *His countenance, like richest alchemy.* Casca sees Brutus's support in terms of alchemical practice, the aim of which was to turn base metals into gold. Shakespeare took the idea from Plutarch: 'to have a man of such estimation as Brutus, to make every man boldly think that by his only presence the fact were holy and just' (*Brutus*, page 111); however, the image here is more appropriate in that both Brutus's favour and alchemy were unsuccessful in their operation.

162   *conceited.* The pun is on (1) 'understood', (2) 'expressed in metaphorical language'.

II.1   (stage direction) *orchard* garden

2   *the progress of the stars* the position which the stars have arrived at in their movement across the sky

5   *When . . . What.* Both words were often used as exclamations of impatience.

7   *taper* candle

11   *no personal cause* no self-interested reason
       spurn at kick against

12   *for the general* for the common political good

13   *the question* the point at issue; compare *Hamlet*, III.1.56 'To be, or not to be – that is the question.'

171

14   *It is the bright day that brings forth the adder* (favourable conditions bring out the latent evil in people)

15   *craves* calls for, requires

17   *do danger* create harm

18-19   *Th'abuse of greatness is when it disjoins | Remorse from power* high authority is misused when its power is exercised without compassion

20-21   *when his affections swayed | More than his reason* when he acted under the influence of his emotions rather than his judgement

21   *a common proof* a matter of common knowledge

22   *That lowliness is young ambition's ladder* that an appearance of humility is the way by which the ambitious man climbs to power. Plutarch makes this point about Caesar on several occasions: for example, 'the people loved him marvellously also, because of the courteous manner he had to speak to every man and to use them gently' (*Caesar*, page 23); and 'But to win himself the love and good will of the people . . . he made common feasts again and general distribution of corn' (ibid., page 78).

24   *upmost round* highest rung

26   *base degrees.* This refers to both the lower steps of the ladder and, by transference, the means employed in the early stages of his career; the pun is on 'base'.

28   *prevent* frustrate by taking anticipatory action

28-9   *since the quarrel | Will bear no colour for the thing he is* since the accusation has no validity considering what Caesar is at this moment

30   *Fashion it thus* let us put the case in this way

31   *these and these extremities* such and such tyrannical extremes

33   *as his kind* according to the nature of its species
        mischievous harmful

35   *closet* study

37   *This paper.* See note to I.3.142-6.

40   *ides.* The Folio text reads 'first' which is clearly an error, probably due to the compositor reading the

abbreviation 'js' (for 'ides') as '1st'. That the error is not Shakespeare's is clear from line 59. Some editors have argued that the Folio reading indicates Brutus's absent-mindedness in practical matters; but this is implausible in view of his reply in line 60.

44   *exhalations* meteors (which were thought to be caused by the earth's exhaling vapours under the influence of the sun's heat)

    whizzing. Fireworks were sometimes used on the Elizabethan stage for effects, and may have been employed here.

46   *'Brutus, thou sleep'st : awake, and see thyself.* See note to I.3.142–6.

52   *under one man's awe* in awe of a single man

53   *ancestors.* See note to I.2.158.

56–8   *O Rome . . . Brutus.* This is Brutus's moment of decision that Caesar's death is a political necessity; his debate is forgotten in the face of Cassius's manufactured 'Roman' pleas.

58   *Thy full petition.* Brutus pledges himself to do all that Rome asks of him: speaking, striking, and thus redressing.

59   *fifteen days.* Some editors change this to 'fourteen days' on the grounds that this scene takes place on the night of the fourteenth; but it is obviously near dawn of the fifteenth; see lines 101–11.

61–2   *Since Cassius first did whet me against Caesar,* | *I have not slept.* These lines suggest a lapse of time between this scene and I.2 in which Brutus has wrestled with his conscience. The historical time was actually one month; but Shakespeare is telescoping the action for reasons of dramatic pace. The passage is based on Plutarch's description: 'either care did wake him against his will when he would have slept, or else oftentimes of himself he fell into such deep thoughts of this enterprise, casting in his mind all the dangers that might happen' (*Brutus*, pages 116–17).

64   *first motion* initial impulse

65   *phantasma* nightmare

66–7   *The genius and the mortal instruments | Are then in council* man's guiding spirit is in violent debate with his passions. This soul and body duel was a common Renaissance idea.

67–8   *state of man, | Like to a little kingdom.* The human organism is viewed as corresponding on the personal level with the body politic. The Folio reading 'of a man' obscures this idea.

70   *your brother Cassius.* Plutarch notes that Brutus and Cassius 'were allied together. For Cassius had married Junia, Brutus' sister' (*Brutus*, page 108).

73   *hats.* Shakespeare was obviously thinking of Elizabethan hats; although the Romans did have various kinds of head-gear.

75   *discover* identify

76   *favour* appearance

79   *are most free* most freely wander about

81–2   *conspiracy; | Hide it in smiles and affability.* See note to lines 225–7.

83   *For if thou path, thy native semblance on* for, if you pursue your way, showing yourself in your true colours. There is no need to emend *path* as many editors have done, as its meaning 'to go along or tread (a way)' is well substantiated by contemporary quotations.

84   *Erebus.* The dark region between the earth and Hades which was crossed by the souls of the dead.

85   *prevention.* See note to line 28.

86   *upon your rest* in disturbing your sleep

87   *do we trouble you?* This is ironical in view of Brutus's mental state prior to the conspirators' entrance.

98   *watchful cares* worries causing sleeplessness

101–11 *Here lies . . . directly here.* This is a fine example of Shakespeare's ability to make a short passage perform a variety of functions. It is, in stage terms, a device to cover the whispered discussion between Brutus and

Cassius; it reminds the audience of the gradual drawing on of the day on which Caesar is to be assassinated; it is symbolically appropriate that Casca should point his sword at the Capitol where Caesar is to be stabbed first by Casca; and it is psychologically true that men at moments of suspense often talk of trivialities to keep their minds from the immediate tension.

104   *fret* adorn with an interlacing pattern

107   *growing* encroaching

108   *Weighing* considering

114   *No, not an oath.* This is the first of Brutus's many impositions of his will on Cassius. Shakespeare deliberately changes Plutarch's account in making only Brutus demur: 'having never taken oaths together nor taken or given any caution or assurance, nor binding themselves one to another by any religious oaths, they all kept the matter so secret to themselves' (*Brutus*, page 115).

       the face of men. The Folio reading may stand although many editors suggest 'faith' as an emendation, owing to Plutarch's phrase 'The wonderful faith and secrecy of the conspirators of Caesar's death' which is printed in the margin beside the passage dealing with the fact that the conspirators did not take an oath. The phrase as it stands comes naturally from Brutus who has been brooding on the appearance of things and their reality, the reluctance of the conspiracy to show its face, and the muffled faces of the plotters. I take it to mean 'the expression on men's faces' (due to their consciousness of the time's evils).

115   *sufferance* suffering, distress

       time's abuse corruption (by Caesar) in these days

116   *betimes* at once

117   *his idle bed* the bed in which he is idle (or, possibly, his unused bed)

118   *high-sighted tyranny.* The reference is to falconry, and Caesar is being viewed as the high-flying bird looking

down on its prey. There may also be the sense of a tyranny which aims at unlimited power. Flavius sees Caesar in similar terms at I.1.72-5.

119 *by lottery* by chance, according to the chance displeasure of the tyrant

124 *prick* spur, encourage

125 *Than secret Romans that have spoke the word* than the fact that we are Romans who, once we have given our word, can be trusted to hold our tongues. See also the note to line 114.

126 *palter* deceive, equivocate

127 *honesty to honesty engaged* words of honour exchanged

129 *cautelous* crafty, deceitful

130 *carrions.* This is a term of contempt: 'men who are no better than dead bodies'.

133 *even* uniform, steadfast

134 *insuppressive* indomitable

138 *guilty of a ... bastardy* guilty of an act that shows illegitimate (that is, non-Roman) blood
several individual, separate

141 *sound him* find out his feelings in this affair

145 *opinion* reputation

148 *no whit* not at all

150 *break with him* broach the matter to him

151-2 *For he will never follow anything | That other men begin.* Shakespeare changes Plutarch's account of this decision to make Brutus the only dissenter:

> *For this cause they durst not acquaint Cicero with their conspiracy, although he was a man whom they loved dearly and trusted best. For they were afraid that he being a coward by nature, and age also having increased his fear, he would quite turn and alter all their purpose, and quench the heat of their enterprise ... seeking by persuasion to bring all things to such safety as there should be no peril (Brutus, page 114).*

153 *Indeed he is not fit.* Contrast this with line 143.

155   *urged* suggested, recommended

156–91 *Mark Antony . . . hereafter*. Plutarch cites this decision
       as Brutus's first fault, but gives different reasons for it:

> *First, . . . it was not honest. Secondly, because . . . there
> was hope of change in him; for . . . Antonius, being a
> noble-minded and courageous man, when he should
> know that Caesar was dead, would willingly help his
> country to recover her liberty (Brutus, pages* 124–5).

158   *shrewd contriver* malicious intriguer
       means capacity

159   *improve* make good use of

160   *annoy* injure, harm
       prevent forestall

164   *Like wrath in death, and envy afterwards*. That is, the
       assassination would appear to be the product of personal
       rather than public motives. This motive is found in
       Plutarch's *Antonius*: 'Brutus would in no wise consent
       to it, saying that venturing on such an enterprise as
       that, for the maintenance of law and justice, it ought to
       be clear from all villainy' (pages 187–8).
       envy hatred, malice

165   *limb of Caesar* a man dependent upon Caesar for any
       importance

167   *spirit of Caesar* (what Caesar represents, 'Caesarism')

168   *spirit* soul

169–70 *O, that we then could come by Caesar's spirit,* | *And not
       dismember Caesar!* This is, of course, tragic irony in
       that Brutus does 'dismember Caesar', but does not
       thereby either lay Caesar's spirit, which appears to him
       in IV.3, or defeat the Caesarian principle, which he
       recognizes as triumphant just before his death at
       V.3.94–6.

169   *come by* get possession of

171   *gentle* noble

173–4 *Let's carve him as a dish fit for the gods,* | *Not hew him as
       a carcass fit for hounds*. Shakespeare probably derived

the hunting imagery associated with Caesar's death in the play from Plutarch: 'Caesar ... was hacked and mangled among them, as a wild beast taken of hunters' (*Caesar*, page 94). Compare similar references at II.2.78-9; III.1.106-11, 204-10.

173   *carve* cut up ceremoniously

176   *servants* emotions, feelings

177-8   *This shall make | Our purpose necessary, and not envious.* This will make it plain that the murder is one of political necessity and not the result of personal rancour.

180   *purgers* those who heal (originally by bleeding and purging the patient)

184   *ingrafted* deep-rooted

186   *all* all the injury

187   *take thought* succumb to melancholy (induced by sorrow)

188   *were much he should* would be far too much to expect from someone like him

188-9   *for he is given | To sports, to wildness, and much company.* Plutarch has a long account of Antony's wildness in *Antonius*, pages 183-4. See the other allusions at I.2.202-3; II.2.116-17; V.1.62.

190   *no fear in him* no reason for fear so far as he is concerned

191   (stage direction) *A clock strikes.* This is anachronistic in that striking clocks were not invented until the thirteenth century and were very popular in Shakespeare's day. What is more important here is that the stage direction reminds the audience forcibly of the passage of time towards the moment of the assassination.

194   *Whether.* This is pronounced here 'whe'r'.

195-6   *For he is superstitious grown of late, | Quite from the main opinion he held once.* There is no mention in Plutarch of Caesar's superstition, nor that he was a follower of Epicurus in ignoring omens and portents.

196   *Quite from the main opinion* at odds with the strongly-held belief

197   *fantasy* imaginings

197   *ceremonies* portents, omens

198   *apparent* manifest

200   *augurers.* These were religious officials who predicted future events and gave advice on public affairs in accordance with the omens they obtained from sacrifice, bird-flight, et cetera.

204   *unicorns may be betrayed with trees.* One method of capturing this legendary beast was for its prey to stand before a tree to persuade it to charge, and then to dodge behind the tree in which the unicorn's horn would stick.

205   *bears with glasses.* A mirror was supposed to be effective in bewildering wild animals by showing them their own image.

       elephants with holes. Like other animals, elephants were trapped by means of specially prepared pits.

206   *toils* snares, traps

       men with flatterers. Decius's point is that dangerous men like dangerous animals can be rendered harmless by the use of cunning.

210   *give his humour the true bent* influence his nature in the right direction

212   *all of us.* It is noticeable, however, that according to the stage direction at II.2.108, Cassius is not present.

213   *uttermost* latest time

215–16   *Caius Ligarius doth bear Caesar hard,* | *Who rated him for speaking well of Pompey.* Compare:

> *Now amongst Pompey's friends there was one called Caius Ligarius, who had been accused unto Caesar for taking part with Pompey, and Caesar discharged him. But Ligarius thanked not Caesar so much for his discharge, as he was offended with him for that he was brought in danger by his tyrannical power. And therefore in his heart he was alway his mortal enemy, and was besides very familiar with Brutus* (Plutarch's *Brutus,* page 113).

215   *bear Caesar hard* feel enmity toward Caesar

216   *rated* rebuked

218   *go along by him* call at his house

220   *fashion him* talk him into joining our party

225-7   *Let not ... constancy.* This is based on Plutarch's remark that Brutus 'did so frame and fashion his countenance and looks that no man could discern he had anything to trouble his mind' (*Brutus*, page 116). The reference to actors here retaining their facial composure is anachronistic because Roman actors wore masks.

225   *put on our purposes* betray our plans

226   *bear it* carry it off

227   *formal constancy* dignified composure

231   *figures ... fantasies* imaginings

233-309   *Brutus, my lord ... with haste.* In this exchange Shakespeare follows both the ideas and the words of a long passage in Plutarch quite closely; see *Brutus*, pages 116-19.

237   *ungently* disrespectfully

240   *arms across.* The conventional Elizabethan attitude for someone absorbed in melancholy brooding.

246   *wafture* waving gesture

249   *withal* moreover

250   *an effect of humour* a symptom of some momentary mood

251   *his* its

254   *condition* frame of mind

255   *know you Brutus* recognize you as Brutus. Some editors emend this to 'know you, Brutus' which weakens its force. The point of Portia's speech is that the description of Brutus is so out of keeping with the Brutus everyone knows and is consequently a measure of his disturbed state of mind.

259   *come by* obtain

261   *physical* healthy

262   *unbracèd.* See note to I.3.48.

       humours dampness

266   *tempt* risk

266 *rheumy and unpurgèd air* air which causes rheum and from which the sun has not drawn the moisture. Fear of fog as a cause of diseases was common at the time.

268 *sick offence* harmful sickness

269 *my place* my being your wife

271 *charm* entreat, conjure

273 *incorporate* make one body. Shakespeare has in mind the Christian rather than the Roman marriage-service.

274 *half* wife

275 *heavy* doleful

281–3 *Is it excepted I should know no secrets | That appertain to you? Am I your self | But, as it were, in sort or limitation.* These are all legal terms connected with the holding of land, and were probably suggested by the word 'bond' in line 280.

285 *suburbs.* The London brothels were located in the suburb of Southwark. The idea is continued in the phrase 'Brutus' harlot' which comes from Plutarch's 'like a harlot'.

289–90 *the ruddy drops | That visit my sad heart.* According to Elizabethan medical theory, the blood was manufactured by the liver and flowed to the heart where it was purified and pumped round the body. Sadness was believed to drain the heart of blood.

295 *Cato's daughter.* Marcus Porcius Cato was Brutus's uncle as well as his father-in-law. His character and career were similar in broad outline to his nephew's: he was an orator and statesman and famous for his rigid moral code; he fought against Caesar with Pompey, and, after Pompey's death, continued to fight in Africa. He made a final resistance at Utica where he committed suicide rather than be captured.

299 *made strong proof of my constancy* put my powers of resolution to a severe test. This is based on Plutarch:

> *loving her husband well, and being of a noble courage, as she was also wise – because she would not ask her husband*

> *what he ailed before she had made some proof by her self – she took a little razor such as barbers occupy to pare men's nails, and, causing her maids and women to go out of her chamber, gave her self a great gash withal in her thigh, that she was straight all of a gore-blood; and, incontinently after, a vehement fever took her, by reason of the pain of her wound* (Brutus, page 118).

307   *construe* elucidate, interpret (accent on first syllable)

308   *charactery* what is written (in the furrows) (accent on second syllable)

311   *Caius Ligarius.* Both Plutarch and Shakespeare are historically wrong as the conspirator was actually Quintus Ligarius. To build up his picture of the well-beloved Brutus, as well as for obvious practical reasons, Shakespeare makes the sick Ligarius visit Brutus rather than vice versa as in Plutarch:

> *Brutus . . . went to see him being sick in his bed, and said unto him: 'O Ligarius, in what a time art thou sick!' Ligarius rising up in his bed and taking him by the right hand, said unto him: 'Brutus,' said he, 'if thou hast any great enterprise in hand worthy of thyself, I am whole'* (Brutus, page 113).

312   *how?* how are you?

313   *Vouchsafe* deign to accept

315   *wear a kerchief.* It was a common practice in Elizabethan England for the sick to wear a cloth round the head.

322   *Brave* noble

323   *exorcist* one who conjures up (and exorcizes) spirits

324   *mortifièd* which was dead

327   *whole* sound, healthy. See Cassius's similar parallel between political and bodily sickness at I.2.253–4.

328   *make sick* kill

331   *To whom* to the dwelling of him to whom

331   *Set on* advance

332   *new-fired* rekindled (with life and courage)

II.2   (stage direction) *night-gown* dressing-gown

2-3   *Thrice hath Calphurnia in her sleep cried out,* | *'Help, ho !* *They murder Caesar!'* Plutarch is less specific about Calphurnia's utterance: 'he heard his wife Calpurnia, being fast asleep, weep and sigh and put forth many fumbling lamentable speeches. For she dreamed that Caesar was slain, and that she had him in her arms' (*Caesar*, page 88).

5   *present* immediate

6   *opinions of success* judgements on the outcome (whether good or bad)

9   *You shall not stir out of your house today.* This is based on Plutarch: 'she prayed him if it were possible not to go out of the doors that day' (*Caesar*, page 89).

10   *Caesar shall forth.* Caesar shall go forth. It is noteworthy that Caesar uses the third person even in talking to his wife.

13   *stood on ceremonies* attached much importance to omens. The detail is derived from Plutarch: 'Calpurnia until that time was never given to any fear or superstition' (*Caesar*, page 89).

16-24 *horrid sights . . . streets.* All these portents are Shakespeare's own invention, unlike those recounted at I.3.15-32, most of which he took from Plutarch. It has been suggested that this account may have been based on some popular version of the prodigies which preceded the destruction of Jerusalem. Shakespeare gives a similar account to this later in *Hamlet*, I.1.113-20:

> *In the most high and palmy state of Rome,*
> *A little ere the mightiest Julius fell,*
> *The graves stood tenantless, and the sheeted dead*
> *Did squeak and gibber in the Roman streets;*

> As, stars with trains of fire, and dews of blood,
> Disasters in the sun; and the moist star
> Upon whose influence Neptune's empire stands
> Was sick almost to doomsday with eclipse.

16   *watch*. An anachronism since there was no night guard in Rome until the reign of Augustus. Shakespeare obviously has in mind the watches of Elizabethan London of which he gives a comic picture in *Much Ado About Nothing*.

19   *fought*. The Folio reading 'fight' is out of sequence with the other tenses in the passage. However, Shakespeare may have deliberately used the dramatic present mixed with the past tense to suggest Calphurnia's excited state.

20   *right form of war* in regular battle-order

22   *hurtled* clashed

23   *did neigh*. The Folio has 'do neigh'; see note to line 19.

25   *beyond all use* outside all normal experience

29   *Are to* are as applicable to

30–31   *When beggars die, there are no comets seen;* | *The heavens themselves blaze forth the death of princes*. This was a common belief in Elizabethan England based ultimately on the series of sympathetic correspondences which were perceived between various levels of life and matter in the universe.

31   *blaze forth* proclaim

32–7   *Cowards die . . . will come*. This speech is based on only a hint from Plutarch: 'And when some of his friends did counsel him to have a guard for the safety of his person . . . he would never consent to it, but said, it was better to die once than always to be afraid of death' (*Caesar*, page 78). Compare this sentiment with Brutus's acceptance of death at III.1.99.

38–40   *They would . . . the beast*. In Plutarch it is only after Calphurnia's plea that Caesar 'would search further of the soothsayers by their sacrifices' that 'the soothsayers, having sacrificed many beasts one after another, told him that none did like them' (*Caesar*, page 89). Shakespeare uses Plutarch's earlier description of Caesar's own sacrifice when he 'found that one of the beasts which was sacrificed had no heart' (page 87).

46   *We are.* The Folio reading 'we heare' would appear to be an error of paleographical origin. However, its appearance in the three subsequent Folio editions of the plays may suggest that Shakespeare was using 'hear' in the sense of 'to be styled as, to pass for'.

49   *consumed in confidence* destroyed by over-confidence

55   *Mark Antony shall say I am not well.* Plutarch has: 'he determined to send Antonius to adjourn the session of the Senate' (*Caesar*, page 89).

56   *And for thy humour I will stay at home.* Plutarch also has Caesar indulging Calphurnia's whim: 'for that he saw her so troubled in mind with this dream she had' (*Caesar*, page 89).

     (stage direction) 'Decius Brutus, surnamed Albinus, in whom Caesar put such confidence that in his last will and testament he had appointed him to be his next heir, and yet was of the conspiracy' (Plutarch's *Caesar*, pages 89–90).

59   *fetch* escort, accompany

60   *happy time* opportune moment

75   *stays* keeps

76–9   *She dreamt . . . in it.* In Plutarch, Calphurnia's dream is different: 'she dreamed that . . . the Senate having set upon the top of Caesar's house, for an ornament . . ., a certain pinnacle . . . she saw it broken down' (*Caesar*, pages 88–9). Shakespeare's invention of the statue spouting blood is the more effective in that it is taken up verbally by the reference to Pompey's statue at III.2.189–90, and physically by the action of the conspirators bathing their hands in Caesar's blood.

76   *tonight* last night

     statue. This is pronounced with three syllables here as it is at III.2.189.

78   *lusty* vigorous

80   *And these does she apply for warnings and portents.* As it stands this line is Alexandrine; it may, however, have occurred owing to the compositor's accidentally reproducing the 'And' from the following line. The accent in 'portents' is on the final syllable.

       apply for interpret as

88   *press* crowd around

89   *For tinctures, stains, relics, and cognizance.* Ironically Decius sees the Romans treating Caesar as a martyr and staining their handkerchiefs in his blood for relics. Antony makes the same point to the mob at III.2.134–8. 'Tinctures' may carry overtones of the alchemical meaning: 'A supposed spiritual principle or immaterial substance whose character or quality may be infused into immaterial things, which are said to be tinctured.'

93–9   *The Senate ... dreams.* This part of Decius's plea is taken straight from Plutarch:

> he ... reproved Caesar, saying that he gave the Senate occasion to mislike with him, and that they might think he mocked them, considering that ... they were ready willingly to grant him all things, and to proclaim him king of all the provinces of the Empire of Rome out of Italy ... and furthermore, that if any man should tell them from him they should depart for that present time, and return again when Calpurnia should have better dreams—what would his enemies and ill-willers say ...? (*Caesar*, pages 90–91).

96–7   *it were a mock | Apt to be rendered* it would be a sarcastic remark likely to be passed

102–3   *my dear dear love | To your proceeding* my deep personal concern for your career

104   *And reason to my love is liable* my affection prompts me to utter what my reason tells me is too outspoken

108   (stage direction) *Enter Brutus, Ligarius, Metellus, Casca, Trebonius, Cinna, and Publius.* See note to II.1.212.

108   *Publius.* Plutarch makes no mention of a conspirator o^f this name, but Shakespeare may have recalled Publius Silicius who was sentenced to death by the Triumvirate and was fond of Brutus.

112–13 *Caesar was ne'er so much your enemy | As that same ague which hath made you lean.* See note to II.1.215–16.

116   *See! Antony, that revels long a-nights.* See note to I.2.202–3.

118   *prepare within.* This is an order directed to servants to set out the wine.

124–5 *And so near will I be | That your best friends shall wish I had been further.* This is inconsistent with the events of the assassination, for Trebonius's task is to draw Antony out of the Capitol, so he does not stab Caesar; see III.1.25–6.

126–7 *Good friends, go in, and taste some wine with me; | And we, like friends, will straightway go together.* Shakespeare employs the classic symbol of betrayal: the murderers taking wine with the victim just before the killing.

128–9 *That every like is not the same, O Caesar, | The heart of Brutus earns to think upon.* By making Brutus comment on the gulf between the appearance of their friendship and the reality of their enmity, Shakespeare shows his consciousness of his personal betrayal.

129   *earns* grieves, yearns

II.3   (stage direction) *Artemidorus.* Compare:

> ... *one Artemidorus also, born in the isle of Gnidos, a doctor of rhetoric in the Greek tongue, who by means of his profession was very familiar with certain of Brutus' confederates and therefore knew the most part of all their practices against Caesar, came and brought him a little bill written with his own hand, of all that he meant to tell him* (Plutarch's *Caesar*, page 91).

1–5   *Caesar, beware ... Caesar.* Shakespeare may have taken the idea for the form of this letter from the account of Caesar given in *A Mirror for Magistrates*: 'Presenting me a scroll of every name; and their whole device.'

5   *bent* directed

6   *If thou beest not immortal.* This is ironical coming at this point in the play; but it does also help to build up a picture of how Caesar was viewed by some Romans. *look about you* take care

6–7   *security gives way to conspiracy* overconfidence gives opportunity for treason. This is an admirable comment on the action of II.2.

8   *lover* devoted friend

11   *as a suitor* pretending to be a petitioner

13   *Out of the teeth of emulation* beyond the reach of envious rivalry

15   *contrive* conspire

II.4   This scene is based on the following passage in Plutarch's *Brutus*:

> *Portia being very careful and pensive for that which was to come and being too weak to away with so great and inward grief of mind, she could hardly keep within, but was frighted with every little noise and cry she heard, . . . asking every man that came from the market-place what Brutus did, and still sent messenger after messenger, to know what news. At length, Caesar's coming being prolonged . . . , Portia's weakness was not able to hold out any longer, and thereupon she suddenly swounded* (page 121).

6   *constancy* fortitude, self-control

9   *to keep counsel.* So far as the play's action is concerned, Brutus has told Portia his secret, as he promised at II.1.304–8. In fact there has been no time for him to do so.

14   *take good note* observe closely

18   *bustling rumour* confused noise

20   *Sooth* in truth

23   *ninth hour*. This is an anachronism; Shakespeare is using modern not Roman measurements of time.

28–30   *That I . . . himself.* These lines have caused some editors to give the Soothsayer's role in this scene to Artemidorus. However, such a change is unwarranted, as the Soothsayer may be merely intending to warn Caesar again. Also 'feeble man' in line 36 is not applicable to Artemidorus.

35   *praetors*. These were Roman judges of high rank. Brutus, Cassius, and Cinna among the conspirators were praetors, Brutus being the chief justice or *praetor urbanus*. See I.3.142–3 and II.1.49–50.

37   *more void* less crowded

45   *merry* in good spirits

III.1   (stage direction) *Popilius*. Although he is not listed in the Folio stage direction, he speaks at line 13.

1–2   *The ides of March are come. | Ay, Caesar, but not gone.* This exchange is perhaps based on two passages. One is in Plutarch's *Caesar*:

> *Caesar going unto the Senate-house and speaking merrily unto the soothsayer, told him: 'The Ides of March be come.' 'So be they,' softly answered the soothsayer, 'but yet they are not past'* (page 88).

The other is in *A Mirror for Magistrates*:

> (*Quod I*) the Ides of March be come, yet harm is none.
> (*Quod he*) the Ides of March be come, yet th' are not gone.

3   *schedule* document, paper

4–5   *Trebonius doth desire you to o'er-read, | At your best leisure, this his humble suit.* Trebonius has the role later (lines 25–6) of drawing Antony away, and no mention is made of his presenting a suit to Caesar. Decius is

merely suspicious of Artemidorus, and manufactures
an excuse to distract Caesar's attention.

6–10 *O Caesar . . . mad.* In Plutarch Caesar receives the petition and attempts to read it:

> He [*Artemidorus*] *. . . pressed nearer to him and said:*
> '*Caesar, read this memorial to yourself, and that
> quickly, for they be matters of great weight, and touch
> you nearly.*' *Caesar took it of him, but could never read
> it, though he many times attempted it, for the number
> of people that did salute him; but holding it still in his
> hand, keeping it to himself, went on withal into the
> Senate-house* (*Caesar*, page 91).

Perhaps under the influence of the account of the
incident in *A Mirror for Magistrates*, Shakespeare
makes Caesar refuse the paper with a grand gesture
which is consistent with his previous attitudes in the
play.

8 *What touches us ourself shall be last served.* Those things
which concern me personally must be last attended to.
Notice the use of the royal plural indicative of Caesar's
arrogance.

10 *give place* get out of the way

12 (stage direction) *Caesar enters the Capitol, the rest following.* Because it is not known with any certainty how
plays were produced on the Elizabethan stage, it is
impossible to say exactly how the entering of the
Capitol was effected in this scene. However, there is
evidence that there was at the Globe Theatre a large
discovery space at the rear of the stage which may here
have been utilized for the Senate House and the atten-
dant senators, with the front area of the stage being
used for the 'street' in which lines 1–11 take place. In
Plutarch the murder takes place in Pompey's theatre:
'the place where the murder was prepared, and where
the Senate were assembled, and where also there stood
up an image of Pompey dedicated by himself amongst

other ornaments which he gave unto the Theatre'
(*Caesar*, page 92).

13 *I wish your enterprise today may thrive.* This is taken
from Plutarch's *Brutus*:

> Another Senator, called Popilius Laena, after he had
> saluted Brutus and Cassius more friendly than he was
> wont to do, he rounded softly in their ears and told them:
> '*I pray the gods you may go through with that you have
> taken in hand....*' When he had said, he presently
> departed from them, and left them both afraid that their
> conspiracy would out (page 121).

17 *I fear our purpose is discoverèd.* This is based on
Plutarch's *Brutus*:

> Popilius Laena ... went unto Caesar and kept him a
> long time with a talk. Caesar gave good ear unto him.
> Wherefore the conspirators..., not hearing what he
> said to Caesar, but conjecturing, by that he had told
> them a little before, that his talk was none other but the
> very discovery of their conspiracy, they were afraid
> every man of them (page 122).

18 *Look how he makes to Caesar: mark him.* In Plutarch's
account Brutus watches Popilius alone and does not
communicate with his companions: 'Brutus marking
the countenance and gesture of Laena, and considering
that he did use himself rather like an humble and
earnest suitor than like an accuser, he said nothing to
his companion' (*Brutus*, page 123).
makes to goes towards

19 *sudden* prompt, quick
prevention being forestalled

20–22 *Brutus, what shall be done? If this be known,* | *Cassius or
Caesar never shall turn back,* | *For I will slay myself.*
Shakespeare took the hint for Cassius's panic from
Plutarch's *Caesar* (page 92): 'But the instant danger of

the present time, taking away his former reason, did suddenly put him into a furious passion and made him like a man half besides himself.' In the account of the assassination in *Brutus* (page 122), Plutarch notes that, rather than be apprehended, should Caesar know of their plan, the conspirators prepare to 'kill themselves with their own hands'.

21   *turn back* return alive

22-4   *Cassius, be constant:* | *Popilius Lena speaks not of our purposes;* | *For look, he smiles, and Caesar doth not change.* In Plutarch, Brutus 'with a pleasant countenance encouraged Cassius. And immediately after, Laena went from Caesar and kissed his hand; which showed plainly that it was for some matter concerning himself that he had held him so long in talk' (*Brutus*, page 123).

22   *constant* unshaken, resolute

24   *Caesar doth not change.* Caesar's expression does not change.

25-6   *Trebonius knows his time; for look you, Brutus,* | *He draws Mark Antony out of the way.* In Plutarch's *Brutus* 'Trebonius ... drew Antonius aside as he came into the house where the Senate sat, and held him with a long talk without' (page 123); in the account of the incident in his *Caesar* it is Decius who does this.

28   *presently* immediately
       prefer present

29   *addressed* ready to do so

32   *Caesar and his senate.* Caesar's arrogance is reflected in the word order he chooses.

35   *prevent* forestall. Caesar knows what Metellus is to ask him; see line 44.

36   *couchings* bowings
       courtesies obeisances

38-9   *And turn pre-ordinance and first decree* | *Into the law of children* and alter by childish whim what has been decreed by time-honoured and pre-ordained law

39   *law.* Although the Folio reading 'lane' has been defended as meaning 'path, by-way', it is usually taken to

be a compositor's error. Other emendations suggested, 'lines' (meaning 'goings-on') and 'lune' (meaning 'whim') are paleographically attractive, but they discontinue the legal metaphor of the previous lines. Recently it has been suggested that the Folio's 'lane' is a variant pronunciation of 'line' which could mean 'rule, canon, precept'.

39–40 *Be not fond,* | *To think* do not be so stupid as to imagine
40 *rebel blood* uncontrollable passions

41–2 *thawed*; *melteth*. Shakespeare is thinking of blood as 'mettle' in the alchemist's crucible; Caesar's blood is thus like gold, in his own eyes, which remains 'true' unlike baser metals. See note to I.2.306–7.

41 *true quality* (the stability proper to it)

43 *spaniel* obsequious (hence flattering)

46 *spurn thee like a cur.* This was perhaps suggested by Plutarch's account of the incident in *Brutus*: 'Caesar at the first simply refused their kindness and entreaties. But afterwards, perceiving they still pressed on him, he violently thrust them from him' (pages 123–4).

47–8 *Know, Caesar doth not wrong, nor without cause* | *Will he be satisfied.* See An Account of the Text, pages 243–4.

51 *repealing* recalling from banishment

53 *Publius Cimber.* The name is Shakespeare's invention; Plutarch gives two accounts of this moment of petition in *Caesar*, pages 92–3, and *Brutus*, pages 123–4. Shakespeare seems to follow the latter more closely: 'one Tullius Cimber ... made humble suit for the calling home again of his brother that was banished. They all made as though they were intercessors for him, and took him by the hands and kissed his head and breast.'

54 *freedom of repeal* permission for his sentence of banishment to be rescinded

58 *be well moved* like to be persuaded to change my decision

59 *If I could pray to move* if I were capable of begging other people to change their minds

60   *constant as the northern star* as unchanging as the pole star

61   *true-fixed* immovable
      resting unchanging

62   *fellow* equal

63   *painted* decorated

67   *apprehensive* capable of reason

69   *holds on his rank* retains his position

70   *Unshaked of motion.* Movement was the law of every star but one.

74   *Wilt thou lift up Olympus?* Will you attempt the impossible? Caesar's choice of words here, and indeed throughout the speech, makes it clear that he is seeing himself as something between a god and a natural force. The effect of the whole speech is to alienate the audience's sympathy from him immediately before the moment he is attacked.

75   *bootless* uselessly, unavailingly

76   *Speak hands for me!* Let the actions of my hands speak for me!

77   *Et tu, Brute?* This is based ultimately on Suetonius's account of Caesar, according to which Caesar, at the moment of death, said to Brutus, 'And thou, my son' – a reference to Suetonius's belief that Brutus was Caesar's illegitimate son. The earliest known appearance of the phrase on the English stage is in *The True Tragedy of Richard Duke of York* (1595), a play believed to be a version of *3 Henry VI*; however, the phrase appears to have been a stage commonplace at the time.
      '*Brute*' is pronounced with two syllables.
      Then fall Caesar! Shakespeare here follows Plutarch's account in *Caesar*:

> Men report also that Caesar did still defend himself against the rest, running every way with his body. But when he saw Brutus with his sword drawn in his hand, then he pulled his gown over his head and made no more resistance (pages 94–5).

80   *pulpits*. This is derived from Plutarch's phrase 'the pulpits for orations' meaning the rostra in the Forum. Shakespeare may have had in mind London's open-air pulpits like that at St Paul's.

81   *enfranchisement*. This was probably suggested by Plutarch's account of the conspirators 'persuading the Romans . . . to take their liberty again' (*Brutus*, page 125).

82–91 *People and senators . . . Publius*. This is Shakespeare's dramatization of Plutarch's description of the panic in the Senate:

> *Brutus, standing in the midst of the house, would have spoken, and stayed the other Senators that were not of the conspiracy, to have told them the reason why they had done this fact. But they, as men both afraid and amazed, fled one upon another's neck in haste to get out at the door . . .* (*Brutus*, page 124).

Instead of general reference, however, Shakespeare effectively focuses the dramatic attention on one aged Senator's reaction to the murder, perhaps suggested by Plutarch's 'they that were present . . . were so amazed with the horrible sight they saw, they had no power to fly . . . not so much as once to make any outcry' (*Caesar*, pages 93–4).

83   *ambition's debt* (that which was due to Caesar's ambition)

86   *mutiny* tumult

89   *Talk not of standing* talk not of organizing resistance. This is in answer to Metellus's suggestion that they defend themselves; and looks ahead to Brutus's miscalculation in III.2 where he again assumes that everyone will understand the assassination when the reasons for it have been explained.

92–5 *And leave us . . . the doers*. This is based on Plutarch's general remark that 'Brutus . . . sent back again the noblemen that came thither with him, thinking it no reason that they, which were no partakers of the murder, should be partakers of the danger' (*Brutus*, page 126).

93   *your age* you as an old man

94   *abide* pay the penalty for

96   *Where is Antony? | Fled to his house amazed.* Shakespeare changes Plutarch's information slightly: 'But Antonius and Lepidus , ... secretly conveying themselves away, fled into other men's houses, and forsook their own' (*Caesar*, page 96).

97–8   *Men, wives, and children stare, cry out, and run, | As it were doomsday.* Plutarch describes the consternation of the citizens at two points: in *Brutus*: 'when the murder was newly done, there were sudden outcries of people that ran up and down the city' (page 125); and in *Caesar*: 'the Senate ... flying filled all the city with marvellous fear and tumult; insomuch as some did shut-to their doors, others forsook their shops and warehouses' (page 96).

99–100   *That we shall die, we know; 'tis but the time | And drawing days out, that men stand upon.* This was a common Elizabethan proverb. Compare Caesar's words at II.2.32–7.

100   *drawing days out* extending the span of life
        stand upon set great store by

101–2   *Why, he that cuts off twenty years of life | Cuts off so many years of fearing death.* Some editors give these lines to Cassius on the grounds of greater appropriateness. However, the change is unnecessary; and the sentiment is similar to that expressed by Casca at I.3.101–2.

105–10   *Stoop ... liberty!* Some editors give these lines to Casca on the grounds that they are inconsistent with Brutus's character. I think they are quite in keeping with his idealistic nature, to which the appeal of such a symbolic action would be irresistible, particularly in view of the way he views the murder at II.1.171–4. The scene also fulfils Calphurnia's prophetic dream in II.2. The whole incident shows Shakespeare taking a vivid detail from Plutarch and giving it a quite different interpretation:

> Then the conspirators thronging one upon another because every man was desirous to have a cut at him, so many swords and daggers lighting upon one body, one of them hurt another; and among them Brutus caught a blow on his hand, because he would make one in murdering of him, and all the rest also were every man of them bloodied (Brutus, page 124; see also Caesar, page 95).

108   *market-place* (the Roman Forum)

109–10   *And waving our red weapons o'er our heads, | Let's all cry, 'Peace, freedom, and liberty!'* This is based on Plutarch's *Brutus*: 'Brutus and his consorts, having their swords bloody in their hands, went straight to the Capitol, persuading the Romans, as they went, to take their liberty again' (page 125).

113   *accents* languages

114   *How many times shall Caesar bleed in sport* how many times (in the future) shall Caesar be killed for entertainment (in plays). This is a common device of Shakespeare's to reinforce the verisimilitude of his historical action by referring to theatrical versions of it; compare *Antony and Cleopatra*, V.2.215–20:

> the quick comedians
> Extemporally will stage us, and present
> Our Alexandrian revels; Antony
> Shall be brought drunken forth, and I shall see
> Some squeaking Cleopatra boy my greatness
> I'th'posture of a whore.

115   *on Pompey's basis.* The irony of this is brought out fully in Plutarch's account: '[Caesar] was driven . . . against the base whereupon Pompey's image stood, which ran

all of a gore-blood till he was slain. Thus it seemed that the image took just revenge of Pompey's enemy, being thrown down on the ground at his feet and yielding up his ghost there' (*Caesar*, page 95).

basis pedestal

along stretched out

117 *knot* party of men joined in conspiracy

120-21 *Brutus shall lead, and we will grace his heels | With the most boldest and best hearts of Rome.* This is based on Plutarch's *Brutus*: 'Brutus went foremost, very honourably compassed in round about with the noblest men of the city' (page 126).

120 *grace* do honour to

122 *Soft* wait a moment

A friend of Antony's. In Plutarch it is Antony who invites the conspirators to come down from the Senate House to visit him, and 'sent them his son for a pledge' (*Brutus*, page 127).

126 *honest* honourable

127 *royal* nobly munificent

129 *feared.* Antony politicly places this word with 'Caesar' and thus half aligns himself with the conspirators; its equally skilfully chosen counterpoise is 'love Brutus'.

136 *Thorough.* This is a common two-syllable form of 'through'.

this untrod state this still unknown set of circumstances

140 *so* if it should

142 *presently* at once

143 *to* as a

144 *a mind* a presentiment

145-6 *still | Falls shrewdly to the purpose* always turns out to be uncomfortably close to what actually happens

146 (stage direction) *Enter Antony.* In Plutarch Antony first meets the conspirators the day following the murder at a meeting of the Senate. By making Antony meet Brutus and the rest immediately after Caesar's death, Shakespeare both speeds up the events and makes

Antony the more striking character in his boldness and craftiness.

152   *be let blood*. This was a medical term referring to the removal of superfluous blood for curative reasons. However, it is here used to mean 'be put to death'.

rank swollen with disease. Antony continues his medical metaphor.

157   *bear me hard*. See note to II.1.215.

158   *purpled* reddened with blood

159   *Fulfil your pleasure*. This is ironic.

Live if I should live

160   *apt* prepared, ready

161   *so* so well, so much

mean of death manner of dying

171   *As fire drives out fire*. This was a common Elizabethan proverb.

so pity, pity so pity for the wrongs of Rome has driven out pity for Caesar

174   *Our arms in strength of malice*. For the many emendations which have been suggested see Collations 2 in An Account of the Text. However, the Folio reading preserves and continues the antithesis of the whole speech between the conspirators' bloody appearance and their loving hearts; literally 'our arms which have all the strength which seeming enmity has endowed them with'.

175   *Of brothers' temper* full of brotherly love

177-8   *Your voice shall be as strong as any man's | In the disposing of new dignities*. Cassius is once again far more politically realistic than Brutus, and offers Antony a share in the power which has come to them by their action in exchange for his support.

177   *voice* vote

178   *dignities* high offices of state

181   *deliver* report to

183   *I doubt not of your wisdom*. This is ironic.

188   *my valiant Casca*. This is irony; contrast it with Antony's real opinion at V.1.43-4.

191   *My credit now stands on such slippery ground.* Antony quibbles on (1) his physical position in standing in Caesar's blood, (2) his reputation as Caesar's friend.

192   *conceit* judge

196   *dearer* more keenly

199   *Most noble.* This could apply (1) ironically to 'foes', (2) sincerely to Caesar, (3) scornfully to his own action in shaking the hands which had killed his friend.

202   *to close* to arrive at an agreement

204   *bayed* brought to bay (like a hunted deer)
    hart. For the remainder of this speech, Antony plays on the words 'hart' and 'heart'. Contrast this speech with Brutus's at II.1.173–4, where Brutus specifically wishes to carve Caesar as a dish fit for the gods and not hack him like the carcass of a hunted beast which Antony here depicts.

206   *Signed* marked with, bearing the evidence of
    spoil. This was a hunting term designating the capture of the hunted animal and its distribution to the hounds; by extension, it meant 'slaughter' generally.
    lethe. The pronunciation is with two syllables. This term, originally taken from the name of the river in Hades, the waters of which induced forgetfulness of the past, came to mean loosely 'oblivion'; here its meaning appears to be 'life-blood'.

207–8   *O world, thou wast the forest to this hart; | And this indeed, O world, the heart of thee.* These lines have been questioned as un-Shakespearian; but there are no grounds whatsoever for doubting their genuineness.

213   *modesty* moderation

214   *I blame you not for praising Caesar so.* This is ironical in view of the echo contained in Antony's funeral oration at III.2.75.

215   *compact* agreement (accent on second syllable)

216   *pricked* marked down by a 'prick' or tick

224   *good regard* sound considerations

225   *son of Caesar.* See note to line 77.

229 *pulpit*. See note to line 80.

230 *order of his funeral* the ceremonies arranged for his funeral

231 *You shall, Mark Antony*. In Plutarch the discussion concerning Caesar's funeral took place in the Senate two days after the murder:

> *When this was done, they came to talk of Caesar's will and testament, and of his funerals and tomb. Then Antonius thinking good his testament should be read openly, and also that his body should be honourably buried and not in hugger-mugger, lest the people might thereby take occasion to be worse offended if they did otherwise ... (Brutus, page 127).*

Plutarch also notes that Brutus's decision to allow Antony to speak to the people was his 'second fault ... when he agreed that Caesar's funerals should be as Antonius would have them; the which indeed marred all' (*Brutus*, page 128).

232–5 *You know not ... utter*. Plutarch notes that 'Cassius stoutly spake against it' (*Brutus*, page 127).

236–7 *I will myself into the pulpit first, | And show the reason of our Caesar's death*. Perhaps this is the clearest display in a small compass of Brutus's political weakness, showing (1) his naïve conviction that everyone sees situations as he does, (2) his idealistic belief in the obvious rightness of his cause, (3) his conviction that 'sovereign reason' prevails in all men, and (4) his blindness concerning the nature of man as a political animal.

238 *protest* proclaim

241 *true* fitting, proper

242 *advantage* benefit (by showing our generosity)

243 *fall* happen

257 *tide of times* course of history

260 *dumb mouths*. This is a frequent phrase of Shakespeare's for wounds, particularly those which can 'accuse'; see the passage quoted in the note to III.2.189–90.

262   *A curse shall light upon the limbs of men.* Many emendations have been suggested for the Folio reading 'limbes', the most favoured being 'lives'. However, there is no difficulty in accepting the image of the blood and destruction of civil war afflicting the limbs of men.

264   *cumber* burden

265   *in use* common, customary

268   *quartered* hacked to pieces

269   *with custom of fell deeds* because of the commonness of cruel actions

270   *ranging* roving in search of prey

271   *Ate.* According to Homer, Ate was the daughter of Zeus and the personification of moral blindness or strife. In Shakespeare she is seen as the goddess of discord and mischief. The word is two-syllabled.

272   *confines* regions (accent on second syllable)

273   *Cry havoc.* Antony is here viewing Caesar's spirit as possessing the kingly privilege of the giving of the order for general pillage and slaughter. The idea is taken up from 'monarch's voice' in line 272.

       let slip unleash

       the dogs of war. These are listed by the Prologue in *Henry V*, lines 5–8:

> *Then should the warlike Harry, like himself,*
> *Assume the port of Mars, and at his heels,*
> *Leash'd in like hounds, should famine, sword, and fire*
> *Crouch for employment.*

282   *big* pregnant with sorrow

283   *Passion* sorrow

285   *Is thy master coming?* See note to III.2.268.

286   *lies* lodges

287   *chanced* happened

289   *No Rome of safety.* The pun is on 'Rome' and 'room', which were apparently pronounced in a similar way at the time; compare I.2.155.

292   *try* test

294   *cruel issue* result of cruelty

295   *the which* (the result of my experiment)

297   *Lend me your hand* (that is, to carry out Caesar's body. According to Plutarch Caesar's body was left in the Senate House when the conspirators went out to address the people.)

III.2   (stage direction) *Enter Brutus and later goes into the pulpit.* Brutus actually goes into the pulpit at line 10.

1   *will be satisfied* demand a satisfactory explanation

2   *audience* a hearing

4   *part* divide

7   *public reasons.* This could mean (1) 'reasons concerning the public good', or (2) 'reasons given in public'.

10   *severally* separately

12   *last* end of my address

13–34   *Romans, countrymen ... reply.* Plutarch records that Brutus made a speech immediately following the murder:

> When the people saw him in the pulpit, although they were a multitude of rakehells of all sorts and had a good will to make some stir, yet, being ashamed to do it for the reverence they bare unto Brutus, they kept silence, to hear what he would say. When Brutus began to speak, they gave him quiet audience (*Brutus*, page 126).

However, this takes place on the day of the murder two days before Caesar's funeral, and there is no indication in Plutarch of the content of the speech. Shakespeare fashioned its style of oratory from Plutarch's hint that Brutus in some of his Greek letters 'counterfeited that brief compendious manner of speech of the Lacedaemonians. As ... he wrote unto the Pergamenians in this sort: *I understand you have given Dolabella money: if you have done it willingly, you con-*

*fess you have offended me; if against your wills, show it
then by giving me willingly'* (*Brutus*, page 104).

13   *lovers* dear friends

15   *have respect to mine honour* accept me as an honourable
man. This is, of course, just the quality Antony stresses
for his own purposes in his oration.

16   *Censure* judge

16-17   *your senses* your reason

30   *rude* barbarous, ignorant

37-8   *The question of his death is enrolled in the Capitol.*
Shakespeare was perhaps recalling Plutarch's account
of the meeting of the Senate on the day following the
assassination; see *Brutus*, pages 127-8.

37   *question of* considerations which led to

38   *enrolled* recorded in the archives. There has of course
been no time for this in the play.

38-9   *his glory not extenuated, wherein he was worthy; nor his
offences enforced* his greatness, which was an honourable
attribute, not being devalued, nor his crimes unduly
stressed

43   *place* office, position

45   *lover* friend

50   *ancestors.* See note to I.2.158.

51   *Let him be Caesar.* Shakespeare is perhaps recalling
those Romans in Plutarch 'that desired change and
wished Brutus only their prince and governor above all
other'. The irony of this line stresses the distance between Brutus's high ideals and the mentality of the
people for whose good he has slain Caesar.

58   *Do grace to Caesar's corpse, and grace his speech* show
due respect to Caesar's body, and hear Antony's speech
with courtesy

59   *Tending* relating

64   *public chair* (Plutarch's 'chair or pulpit for orations')

66   *For Brutus' sake* in Brutus's name
beholding indebted

74ff.   *Friends, Romans.* . . . Plutarch gives two brief accounts
of Antony's oration:

*Antonius making his funeral oration in praise of the
dead, according to the ancient custom of Rome, and
perceiving that his words moved the common people to
compassion, he framed his eloquence to make their hearts
yearn the more (Brutus, pages 128-9);*

and

*he made a funeral oration in commendation of Caesar.
... When he saw that the people were very glad and
desirous also to hear Caesar spoken of and his praises
uttered, he mingled his oration with lamentable words,
and by amplifying of matters did greatly move their
hearts and affections unto pity and compassion (Antonius, pages 188-9).*

The only hint for the style of Antony's oration provided by Plutarch is that Antony 'used a manner of
phrase in his speech called Asiatic, which ... was much
like to his manners and life; for it was full of ostentation,
foolish bravery, and vain ambition' (ibid., page 175).

112   *I fear there will a worse come in his place.* This was a
      common Elizabethan saying.

115   *dear abide it* dearly pay the penalty for it

121   *none so poor to do him reverence* the lowest member of
      society is too high to pay his respects to Caesar

122-3 *to stir | Your hearts and minds to mutiny and rage.* This
      is based on Plutarch's remark in *Brutus*: 'the people fell
      presently into such a rage and mutiny' (page 129).

123   *mutiny* disorder, riot

130   *closet* study
      'tis his will. In Plutarch the will of Caesar is first read in
      the Senate the day following Caesar's murder: 'they
      came to talk of Caesar's will and testament ... An-
      tonius thinking good his testament should be read
      openly' (*Brutus*, page 127). He later notes in connexion
      with Brutus's mistakes that 'when Caesar's testament
      was openly read among them, ... the people then loved
      him and were marvellous sorry for him' (ibid., page 128).

205

134   *napkins* handkerchiefs. The reference is to the practice of keeping as relics cloths stained in the blood of martyrs. The idea of hagiolatry may have been suggested to Shakespeare by Plutarch's remark that 'Caesar's funerals should be honoured as a god' (*Caesar*, page 97).

142   *meet* fitting, proper

143   *You are not wood, you are not stones, but men.* Contrast these lines with those of Marullus at I.1.35–6.

150   *stay* wait

151   *o'ershot myself* said more than I intended

168   *far* farther

169   *Bear* move

171–81 *You all ... or no.* Plutarch gives two accounts of this incident – in *Brutus*, page 129, and in *Antonius*, page 189. Shakespeare's version seems more indebted to the latter: 'to conclude his oration, he unfolded before the whole assembly the bloody garments of the dead, thrust through in many places with their swords, and called the malefactors cruel and cursed murderers'; he combines this with an event related in *Caesar* where the citizens 'saw his body ... all bemangled with gashes of swords' (page 97).

174   *That day he overcame the Nervii.* Antony was not in fact with Caesar at this battle, which was fought at Sambre in the winter of 57 B.C. It was one of the most important Roman victories of the Gallic Wars and was likely to be remembered by the Roman people because 'The Senate ... ordained that they should ... keep feasts and solemn processions fifteen days together without intermission, having never made the like ordinance at Rome for any victory that ever was obtained' (*Caesar*, page 41).
       Nervii. In the edition of Plutarch which Shakespeare used there is a marginal note: 'Nervii the stoutest warriors of all Belgae'. The word is three-syllabled.

176   *envious* spiteful

180   *to be resolved* to learn for certain

181   *unkindly.* The quibble is on the two meanings (1) 'cruelly', (2) 'not of kind', meaning 'unnaturally'.

182   *angel* favourite. The word is Plutarch's.

184   *unkindest.* See note to line 181.

189–90   *Even at the base of Pompey's statue,* | *Which all the while ran blood.* For the passage in Plutarch on which this is based see note to III.1.115. Antony may here be contrasting the hard hearts of the conspirators with the 'sympathy' shown by the statue. The Elizabethan audience, however, may have interpreted the phenomenon in the light of the common belief that a murdered man's wounds bled afresh in the presence of his murderer; compare *Richard III*, I.2.55–9:

> O, gentlemen, see, see! Dead Henry's wounds
> Open their congeal'd mouths and bleed afresh.
> Blush, blush, thou lump of foul deformity,
> For 'tis thy presence that exhales this blood
> From cold and empty veins, where no blood dwells.

189   *base* pedestal
      statue. This is pronounced with three syllables here.

193   *flourished.* The quibble is on the two meanings (1) 'triumphed', (2) 'brandished a sword'.

195   *dint* stroke, impression

197   *vesture* mantle

197–8   *Look you here,* | *Here is himself.* See note to lines 171–81.

198   *marred* mangled
      with by

205–6   *Revenge! About! Seek! Burn! Fire! Kill! Slay! Let not a traitor live.* In Plutarch's *Caesar* when the people 'saw his body . . . all bemangled with gashes of swords, then there was no order to keep the multitude and common people quiet' (page 97).

205   *About!* to work!

214   *private griefs* personal grievances

221   *public leave to speak* permission to speak publicly

222–4   *neither wit, nor words, nor worth, | Action, nor utterance, nor the power of speech | To stir men's blood.* Antony lists the qualities of the good orator here: wit (intellectual brilliance); words (fluency); worth (weight of authority); action (gesture and bearing); utterance (delivery); effectiveness; results.

222   *wit.* The Folio reading 'writ' has been defended as referring to a prepared oration; but it seems out of keeping with the rest of the passage.

224   *right on* just as I think, without art

226   *poor poor dumb mouths.* See note to lines 189–90 and to III.1.260.

229   *ruffle up* stir up to anger

243   *To every several man, seventy-five drachmas.* Plutarch refers to Caesar's bequest on three occasions: in *Caesar*, page 97, *Antonius*, page 190, and *Brutus*, page 128, which last is nearest to Shakespeare's line: 'it appeared that he bequeathed unto every citizen of Rome seventy-five drachmas a man'.
     several individual
     drachmas. The drachma was originally a Greek coin.

245   *royal* nobly munificent

249–50   *orchards, | On this side Tiber.* For 'orchards' see note to II.1 (stage direction). Caesar's gardens actually were situated on the other side of the river. Shakespeare follows North, who in his turn was following Amyot's mistranslation of Plutarch's Greek: 'he left his gardens and arbours unto the people, which he had on this side of the river of Tiber (in the place where now the Temple of Fortune is built)' (*Brutus*, page 128).

251   *common pleasures* public parks

255–6   *We'll burn his body in the holy place, | And with the brands fire the traitors' houses.* Plutarch gives three accounts of this incident: in *Caesar*, pages 97–8, *Antonius*, page 189, and *Brutus*, page 129, the last of which is the closest to Shakespeare's words:

> *Others plucked up forms, tables, and stalls about the*
> *market-place ... and having laid them all on a heap*
> *together, they set them on fire, and thereupon did put the*
> *body of Caesar, and burnt it in the middest of the most*
> *holy places. And furthermore, when the fire was*
> *thoroughly kindled, some here, some there, took burning*
> *fire-brands, and ran with them to the murderers' houses*
> *that had killed him, to set them a-fire.*

255   *holy place* (where the most sacred temples were situated)
259   *Pluck down* tear loose
260   *windows* shutters
263   *fellow*. This was a term often used either contemptuously
      or to inferiors.
264   *Octavius is already come to Rome*. Historically it was six
      weeks after Caesar's funeral that Octavius returned to
      Rome from Apollonia. As elsewhere in the play,
      Shakespeare is compressing historical time for greater
      dramatic effect.
267   *straight* at once
268   *upon a wish* exactly as I desired. In Plutarch it is
      Lepidus who enters Rome the night following the
      assassination. Antony at first 'made no reckoning of'
      Octavius because he was young, but later viewed him as
      a rival. It was only in the autumn of the year after the
      assassination that Octavius and Antony settled their
      differences. Shakespeare foreshortens these events for
      dramatic purposes, by establishing the Triumvirate
      immediately after Caesar's funeral, and only hints at
      the antagonism between Antony and Octavius in IV.1
      and V.1.
270–71 *I heard him say Brutus and Cassius | Are rid like madmen*
      through the gates of Rome. Plutarch has in *Antonius*:
      'Brutus . . . and his accomplices, for safety of their
      persons, were driven to fly the city' (pages 189–90).
272–3 *some notice of the people, | How I had moved them* some
      information about how I had stirred up the people.

Plutarch notes that 'the conspirators, foreseeing the danger before, had wisely provided for themselves' (*Brutus*, page 129).

III.3   (stage direction) *Cinna*. Helvetius Cinna was a poet, and a friend of Catullus. The scene is based on the following passage in Plutarch's *Caesar*:

> *There was one of Caesar's friends called Cinna, that had a marvellous strange and terrible dream the night before. He dreamed that Caesar bade him to supper, and that he refused, and would not go; then that Caesar took him by the hand, and led him against his will. Now Cinna hearing at that time that they burnt Caesar's body in the market-place, notwithstanding that he feared his dream and had an ague on him besides, he went into the market-place to honour his funerals. When he came thither, one of the mean sort asked him what his name was? He was straight called by his name. The first man told it to another, and that other unto another, so that it ran straight through them all that he was one of them that murdered Caesar. For indeed one of the traitors to Caesar was also called Cinna as himself. Wherefore ... they fell upon him with such fury that they presently dispatched him in the market-place* (page 98; see also *Brutus*, pages 129–30).

1   *tonight* last night

2   *unluckily charge my fantasy* load my imaginings with ill omen. It was a common Elizabethan idea that a dream of good cheer boded ill luck for the dreamer. Notice Shakespeare's change of Plutarch.

9   *directly* straightforwardly

17–18 *they are fools that marry*. This was an Elizabethan proverb.

18   *You'll bear me a bang for that*. I shall strike you for that (remark).

20   *Directly.* The pun here is on the two meanings (1) 'straightforwardly', and (2) 'in a straight line'.

25   *Briefly.* The pun is on the two meanings (1) 'in brief', (2) 'recently'.

34   *pluck but his name out of his heart.* This is grotesquely related to Brutus's attempt to destroy the implications of Caesar's spirit or name by killing his body. Compare also Cassius's playing with the names of Brutus and Caesar at I.2.141–6.

       turn him going send him packing

36–8   *Come, brands . . . Ligarius.* See note to III.2.255–6.

IV.1.1–6   *These many . . . damn him.* This exchange is based on Plutarch's *Antonius*:

> And thereupon all three met together (to wit, Caesar, Antonius, and Lepidus). . . . But yet they could hardly agree whom they would put to death; for every one of them would kill their enemies, and save their kinsmen and friends. Yet at length, giving place to their greedy desire to be revenged of their enemies, they spurned all reverence of blood and holiness of friendship at their feet (page 194; see also *Brutus*, page 137).

1   *pricked* marked by a 'prick' on the list

2   *Your brother too must die.* Plutarch notes that 'both of them [Antonius and Octavius] together suffered Lepidus to kill his own brother Paulus. Yet some writers affirm that Caesar and Antonius requested Paulus might be slain, and that Lepidus was contented with it' (*Antonius*, page 194). Lucius Aemilius Paullus had been consul in 50 B.C.; and at Caesar's death joined the republican faction and helped declare Lepidus a public enemy in June 43 B.C. for having joined Antony. After the Triumvirate was formed his name was placed first on the proscriptive list by Lepidus. He escaped to join

Brutus and Cassius, was pardoned after Philippi, but chose to live and die out of Rome.

4 *Publius*. In Plutarch Antony allows his uncle Lucius Caesar to be placed on the list; but he has no nephew Publius. However, immediately prior to the passage dealing with the Triumvirate's condemnations in *Brutus* there is the mention of 'Publius Silicius . . . who . . . was one of the proscripts or outlaws appointed to be slain' (page 137).

6 *with a spot I damn him* with a mark I condemn him to death

9 *cut off some charge* lessen some of the expenditure. Plutarch says that Calphurnia put Antony in charge of Caesar's goods, and notes that the Triumvirs 'were easily agreed and did divide all the Empire of Rome between them, as if it had been their own inheritance' (*Antonius*, page 194). Shakespeare is contrasting Antony's attitude to Caesar's will here with that in III.2 when it was a useful political tool.

12 *slight unmeritable* insignificant and unworthy of consideration

13 *Meet* fitting

14 *three-fold world divided*. This was the Roman world: Europe, Asia, Africa. Antony was to govern Gaul, Lepidus Spain, Octavius Africa, Sardinia, and Sicily.

16 *voice* vote, opinion

17 *black sentence* death sentence

18 *I have seen more days than you*. I am older (thus more experienced) than you. In Plutarch 'Antonius at the first made no reckoning of him, because he was very young; and said he lacked wit and good friends to advise him' (*Antonius*, page 190).

20 *To ease ourselves of divers slanderous loads* to divest ourselves of some of the blame or reproach that may be laid upon us

21 *as the ass bears gold*. This was an Elizabethan proverb: 'An ass is but an ass though laden with gold.'

22 *business* heavy work

26 *empty* unburdened, idle

  to shake his ears. This was a proverbial expression for the only occupation for those who have been dismissed.

27 *in commons* on public pasture lands

28 *soldier.* The word has three syllables here.

30 *appoint* assign

  store a supply

32 *To wind* to turn, to wheel (a term drawn from horsemanship)

33 *His corporal motion governed by my spirit* his physical movements controlled by my mind

34 *in some taste* in some measure, to some degree

36 *barren-spirited* lacking originality or initiative

36–9 *one that ... fashion* one that takes over outdated ideas and worn-out fashions of thought, so that all his ideas are either second-hand or out of date. Compare the picture of Lepidus given in *Antony and Cleopatra*, II.7.

37 *objects* wonders, curiosities

  arts artificial processes

  imitations second-hand ideas

38 *staled* made common or cheap

39 *Begins his fashion* are for him at the height of fashion

40 *a property* a mere tool or belonging for cleverer men to use

41 *Listen* hear

41–2 *Brutus and Cassius | Are levying powers.* This is based on Plutarch's *Brutus*, in which Brutus and Cassius meet at the city of Smyrna and 'were marvellous joyful, and no less courageous when they saw the great armies together which they had both levied ... having ships, money, and soldiers enow, both footmen and horsemen, to fight for the Empire of Rome' (page 138).

42 *straight make head* raise a force immediately

44 *made* made certain

  stretched used to their fullest extent

45 *presently* forthwith

46-7   *How covert matters may be best disclosed,* | *And open*
        perils surest answerèd how hidden plans may be found
        out, and open dangers safely dealt with

48-9   *at the stake,* | *And bayed about with many enemies* tied to
        a stake (like a bear) and surrounded by many enemies
        (like barking dogs eager to attack us). The metaphor
        is from bear-baiting.

51   *mischiefs* schemes to harm us

IV.2   This scene takes place at Sardis; and is based on
        Plutarch's *Brutus*: 'About that time Brutus sent to pray
        Cassius to come to the city of Sardis; and so he did.
        Brutus, understanding of his coming, went to meet him
        with all his friends' (page 145).

        (stage direction) *Enter Brutus, Lucilius. . . .* It is clear
        that this scene takes place before Brutus's tent into
        which he retires with Cassius at line 52, and which may
        have been the large discovery-area at the rear of the
        stage (see note to stage direction at III.1.12). Possibly
        Brutus enters from the tent attended by his servant
        Lucius, and meets Lucilius at the head of his soldiers,
        bringing in Titinius and Pindarus.

        Titinius. It is odd that Brutus ignores Titinius who is
        Cassius's officer; those editors may be right who suggest
        that he enters with Cassius at line 30.

2   *Give the word, ho! and stand!* Lucilius is here passing
        on Brutus's order to his subordinates.

6   *He greets me well* he sends his greetings with a good man

6-9   *Your master ... undone.* 'Now as it commonly hap-
        peneth in great affairs between two persons, both of
        them having many friends and so many captains under
        them, there ran tales and complaints betwixt them'
        (Plutarch's *Brutus*, page 145).

7   *In his own change, or by ill officers* whether from his
        changed feelings towards me, or by the misconduct of
        unworthy subordinates

8	*worthy* justifiable, considerable
8–9	*to wish* | *Things done undone*. This was a proverbial expression.
10	*be satisfied* receive a full explanation
12	*full of regard and honour* meriting all respect and honour
14	*resolved* fully informed
16	*familiar instances* signs of friendship
17	*conference* conversation
19	*Ever note* always observe
21	*an enforcèd ceremony* strained manners
22	*tricks* artifices
23	*hollow* insincere
	hot at hand spirited at the start
24	*mettle* spirit
26	*fall* let fall, lower
	crests ridges of the horse's neck
27	*Sink in the trial* fail when tested
28	*Sardis*. This was the capital city of the ancient kingdom of Lydia in Asia Minor.
29	*horse in general* all the mounted soldiers
31	*gently* slowly
37–41	*Most noble . . . them*. In Plutarch there is no squabble in front of the troops: 'Therefore before they fell in hand with any other matter, they went into a little chamber together, and bade every man avoid, and did shut the doors to them. Then they began to pour out their complaints one to the other' (*Brutus*, page 145).
40	*this sober form* this grave and restrained manner
41	*be content* keep calm. Compare Cassius's lack of restraint and Brutus's calm at III.1.20–22.
42	*griefs* grievances
	I do know you well. Brutus indicates by this that they are old friends and so need not act like enemies.
45–7	*Bid them move away;* | *Then in my tent, Cassius, enlarge your griefs,* | *And I will give you audience*. See Plutarch's words in the note to lines 37–41.

47   *audience* a hearing

48   *their charges* their troops

50, 52   *Lucius, Lucilius.* The Folio reads 'Lucilius' at line 50 and 'Let Lucius' at line 52. The readings are obviously erroneous and need transposing. Lucius, a servant and a boy, and Titinius, Cassius's officer, are ill-paired as guards for the Generals' tent. It is far more appropriate that Lucius carry the message for Brutus (as Pindarus, his counterpart does for Cassius), and that Lucilius make up the guard with Titinius. That this was Shakespeare's intention is demonstrated by the fact that it is Lucilius whom we find on guard at IV.3.126.

IV.3   (stage direction) If the stage arrangement suggested in the note on the first stage direction of IV.2 is accepted, then at this point Brutus and Cassius would withdraw into the rear area of the stage. Titinius and Lucilius would stand guard at one side of the stage, still in view of the audience. The scuffle between them and the poet (at lines 123–7) would take place between the point where they are standing and the stage area representing the interior of the tent.

2   *noted* publicly disgraced, slandered. Plutarch's *Brutus* has: 'Brutus, upon complaint of the Sardians, did condemn and noted Lucius Pella for a defamed person, that had been a Praetor of the Romans and whom Brutus had given charge unto; for that he was accused and convicted of robbery and pilfery in his office' (page 147).

5   *slighted off* slightingly dismissed. A singular ver b with a plural subject is frequent in Shakespeare's grammar.

7–8   *In such a time as this it is not meet | That every nice offence should bear his comment.* Plutarch has: 'This judgement much misliked Cassius. . . . And therefore he greatly reproved Brutus for that he would show himself so strait and severe, in such a time as was meeter

216

to bear a little than to take things at the worst' (*Brutus*, page 147.)

8   *That every nice offence should bear his comment* that every minor offence should be criticized

       his its

10   *condemned to have* accused of having

       itching palm streak of covetousness in your nature. At one point Plutarch contrasts the extreme covetousness and cruelty of Cassius to the Rhodians with Brutus' clemency unto the Lycians (*Brutus*, page 143).

11   *mart* deal in or traffic in

15–16 *The name of Cassius honours this corruption,* | *And chastisement doth therefore hide his head.* The fact that the name of Cassius is connected with corrupt dealings endows them with an unwarranted respectability, so that punishment is impossible (for inferior men as well as for Cassius). This is based on Plutarch's *Brutus*: 'Cassius . . . himself had secretly, not many days before, warned two of his friends, attainted and convicted of the like offences, and openly had cleared them; but yet he did not therefore leave to employ them in any manner of service as he did before' (page 147).

19   *for justice' sake.* This is the first time justice has been instanced as one of the motives for the conspiracy.

20–21 *What villain touched his body, that did stab,* | *And not for justice?* Who of the conspirators was such a villain as to strike Caesar for any other motive than a desire for justice? This is ironical in that it is addressed to Cassius, for we know his motive to have been anything but disinterested.

21   *And not* except

23   *supporting robbers.* There has been no earlier suggestion of this. Its occurrence is due to the fact that Shakespeare is following his source closely at this point:

       Brutus in contrary manner answered that he should remember the Ides of March, at which time they slew

> *Julius Caesar; who neither pilled nor polled the country,
> but only was a favourer and suborner of all them that
> did rob and spoil by his countenance and authority
> (Brutus, page 147).*

25 *the mighty space of our large honours* the high and
honourable offices in our power to confer

26 *trash.* This was a contemptuous term for money.

graspèd thus. This is presumably an indication to the
actor to make an appropriate gesture.

27 *bay the moon* howl against the moon. This was a proverbial expression indicating a useless activity.

28 *bait* worry, harass. Many editors emend this to 'bay';
but there is no need for such a change. The word as it
stands picks up the reference to the dog in the previous
line, as Cassius sees himself as an animal (a bear or
bull) baited by a dog. There may also be a pun on
'bait/bite', for in the sixteenth and seventeenth centuries words which have i + consonant + e in modern
English were often pronounced as a + consonant + e.

30 *hedge me in* limit my authority

31 *Older.* This is derived from Plutarch, who notes 'he was
the elder man' (Brutus, page 138).

32 *make conditions* manage affairs

35 *Urge* drive, provoke

36 *health* safety, welfare

tempt try, provoke

37 *slight* of no worth or importance

39 *way and room* free course and scope

rash choler quick temper

40 *stares* glares

44 *budge* flinch

45 *observe* pay obsequious respect to

crouch bow

46 *testy humour* irascible temper

47 *You shall disgest the venom of your spleen.* I will make you
swallow the poison from your bad temper. The spleen
was believed to be the seat of the emotions.

49   *mirth, yea, for my laughter* an object of fun and ridicule. Compare line 113, and I.2.72.

52   *vaunting* boasting

54   *to learn of* to be instructed by

56   *I said an elder soldier, not a better.* Cassius, in fact, said that he was more experienced and a better planner; see lines 30–32. Also see the note to V.1.18–20.

58   *moved* exasperated, annoyed

59   *tempted.* See note to line 36.

67   *honesty* integrity, uprightness

69   *respect not* ignore

69–70   *I did send to you | For certain sums of gold, which you denied me.* This is based on Plutarch's *Brutus*:

> *Brutus prayed Cassius to let him have some part of his money, whereof he had great store. . . . Cassius' friends hindered this request and earnestly dissuaded him from it, persuading him that it was no reason that Brutus should have the money which Cassius hath gotten together by sparing and levied with great evil will of the people their subjects. . . . This notwithstanding, Cassius gave him the third part of his total sum* (pages 140–41).

75   *indirection* devious, irregular means

80   *rascal counters* trashy coins

84   *rived* split, cleft, broken

91   *Olympus* (the legendary home of the Greek gods)

95   *braved* defied, opposed, challenged

96   *Checked* rebuked, reproved

98   *cast into my teeth.* This was a proverbial expression.

101   *Dearer* more precious

       Pluto's mine. Pluto, the god of the underworld, and Plutus, the god of riches, were frequently confused both in Classical and Elizabethan times.

103   *that denied thee gold.* This seems to contradict line 82; but what Cassius is really implying is that although Brutus will have it that he was denied gold, yet Cassius is ready 'to give my heart', etc.

107   *it shall have scope* your temper shall have free rein

108   *dishonour shall be humour.* I shall take your future insults to be merely the products of a whim.

111–12   *Who, much enforcèd, shows a hasty spark,* | *And straight is cold again.* This was a proverbial expression.

111   *Who* which
        much enforcèd struck with force

112   *straight* at once

114   *blood ill-tempered* ill-balanced nature

117   *What's the matter?* This is not intended sarcastically, but shows genuine sympathy for Cassius's distraught state.

119   *rash humour* irascible temper. The fact that Cassius inherited his quick temper from his mother is Shakespeare's invention; Plutarch merely notes that he was 'marvellous choleric and cruel' (*Brutus*, page 139).
        which my mother gave me which I inherited from my mother

122   *and leave you so* and let it go at that
        (stage direction) *Poet.* In Plutarch he is 'one Marcus Faonius, that had been a friend and follower of Cato while he lived, and took upon him to counterfeit a philosopher not with wisdom and discretion but with a certain bedlam and frantic motion, he would needs come into the chamber, though the men offered to keep him out' (*Brutus*, page 146). See the note on the opening stage direction of this scene.

126   *stay* prevent

129–30   *Love, and be friends, as two such men should be;* | *For I have seen more years, I'm sure, than ye.* 'This Faonius . . . with a certain scoffing and mocking gesture . . . rehearsed the verses which old Nestor said in Homer:

> *My lords, I pray you hearken both to me,*
> *For I have seen moe years than suchie three.*'
>
>   *Brutus*, page 146.

Shakespeare attributes the couplet to Faonius himself, and, on the strength of this attribution, makes him a poet rather than the pseudo-philosopher of Plutarch.

131   *cynic* boorish man

132   *sirrah!* This was a contemptuous form of address.
        Saucy insolent

134   *I'll know his humour, when he knows his time.* I'll put up
        with his kind of behaviour when he keeps it for a proper
        time and place.

135   *jigging* rhyming, versifying

136   *Companion.* Here this is used as a term of contempt
        meaning 'fellow'.

143–4 *Of your philosophy you make no use, | If you give place to
        accidental evils.* As a Stoic Brutus ought not to have
        given way to anger over incidental adversities.

144   *place* way

148   *killing* being killed

149   *touching* grievous

150   *Upon* as a result of

150–54 *Impatient of my absence ... fire.* Some editors have
        suggested the reading 'Impatience' on grammatical
        grounds. However, the syntax of the Folio reading is
        not uncommon in Shakespeare, and it avoids a clash of
        sibilants. Plutarch mentions Portia's death, but not in
        connexion with the quarrel:

> *And for Portia, Brutus' wife, Nicolaus the philosopher
> and Valerius Maximus do write that she, determining
> to kill herself (her parents and friends carefully looking
> to her to keep her from it), took hot burning coals and
> cast them into her mouth, and kept her mouth so close
> that she choked herself (Brutus, page 173).*

152–3 *for with her death | That tidings came.* The news of
        Portia's death and that concerning the strength of
        Antony's and Octavius's forces came together.

162   *taper* candle

163   *call in question* deliberate upon

167–8 *Come down upon us with a mighty power, | Bending their
        expedition toward Philippi.* These lines and lines 194–

210, 223 suggest that both armies are bearing down on Philippi; but in fact Sardis and Philippi are not close together.

168 *Bending* directing

Philippi (accent on second syllable throughout)

169 *tenor* purport

171-6 *That by proscription . . . being one.* This is based on Plutarch's *Brutus*: 'After that, these three, Octavius Caesar, Antonius, and Lepidus . . . did set up bills of proscription and outlawry, condemning two hundred of the noblest men of Rome to suffer death; and among that number Cicero was one' (page 137).

171 *proscription* condemnation to death

179-93 *Had you . . . bear it so.* It is generally believed that these lines constitute a first version of the announcement of Portia's death which was imperfectly deleted in the manuscript from which the Folio text was printed, and that they thus record Shakespeare's first intention of making Brutus display his Stoicism and his ability to subordinate private emotions to public duty. The 'later' version (lines 141-56) shows his gentleness and humanity, accounts in part for his reaction to Cassius, and suggests far more skilfully Brutus dealing with his co-leader while bearing the sorrow of his wife's death. If this theory is correct, then Brutus's 'Well, to our work alive' (line 194) would apply to Cicero's death. Some critics have argued that Shakespeare intended both versions to stand, basing their case on the grounds of their reading of Brutus's character, and of theatrical effectiveness. See An Account of the Text, page 244.

189 *once* some day

192 *have as much of this in art* have as much of this Stoical fortitude in theory

193 *nature* emotions

194 *Well, to our work alive.* Let us get on with the work that is our present concern. The choice of the word 'alive'

has overtones of the importance of matters concerning the living over grief for the dead.

194–223 *What do you think ... Philippi.* This passage is based on Plutarch's *Brutus*:

> Cassius was of opinion not to try this war at one battle, but rather to delay time and to draw it out in length, considering that they were the stronger in money and the weaker in men and armours. But Brutus in contrary manner did alway before, and at that time also, desire nothing more than to put all to the hazard of battle, as soon as might be possible, to the end he might either quickly restore his country to her former liberty, or rid him forthwith of this miserable world, being still troubled in following and maintaining of such great armies together. .... Thereupon it was presently determined they should fight battle the next day (pages 152–3).

199   *offence* harm

201   *of force* necessarily

203   *forced affection* allegiance out of necessity

207   *new-added* reinforced

211–23 *Under your pardon ... at Philippi.* Even as in the matter of Antony's possible assassination, and of his request to speak at Caesar's funeral, Cassius is here overruled against his better judgement. On each of the three occasions Brutus is wrong. Cassius disclaims responsibility for the present erroneous decision at V.1.73–5.

218   *Omitted* neglected, missed

219   *bound in* confined to

222   *ventures* goods risked in trade
      with your will as you wish

226   *niggard* supply sparingly, stint

228   *hence* go from here

229   (stage direction) *Enter Lucius.* In the Folio text, this stage direction appears before line 229, which is printed

223

there as an unbroken line. It is obvious that Lucius is summoned, given the order, and exits.

gown. See note to II.2.0 (stage direction).

237   *instrument* (possibly a lute or a cittern)

239   *Poor knave.* This was a term of endearment, meaning 'poor lad'.

       o'erwatched tired through staying awake

245   *raise* rouse

247   *watch your pleasure* be awake to anything you wish to be done

249   *otherwise bethink me* change my mind

250   *the book.* Plutarch mentions several times Brutus's addiction to reading late into the night; for example, 'if he had any leisure left him, he would read some book till the third watch of the night' (*Brutus*, page 148; see also ibid., page 105).

255   *touch* play on
         strain tune

256   *an't* if it

260   *young bloods* youthful constitutions

264   (stage direction) *Music, and a song.* Shakespeare frequently uses this device to provide a peaceful lull before an emotionally highly-charged moment; see, for example, the use of Desdemona's song in *Othello*, IV.3. In the professional theatre the most frequently used song at this point is 'Orpheus with his lute' from *Henry VIII*, III.1; another appropriate possibility which has been suggested is 'Come, heavy sleep' from John Dowland's *First Book of Songs* (1597).

265   *murderous* (because it is 'The death of each day's life' (*Macbeth*, II.2.38))

266   *leaden mace.* The reference is to the mace or staff which was carried by the serjeant or sheriff's officer, and with which he touched the shoulder of the person to be apprehended.

271   *leaf turned down.* This is anachronistic, since Brutus would be reading from a *liber* or *volumen* which was a scroll.

273-5 *How ill . . . apparition.* It was a common Elizabethan superstition that a light turned dim or blue in the presence of a ghost. Shakespeare is here following Plutarch closely: '. . . looking towards the light of the lamp that waxed very dim, he saw a horrible vision of a man, of a wonderful greatness and dreadful look, which at the first made him marvellously afraid' (*Caesar*, page 100).

274-6 *I think . . . any thing.* Shakespeare seems to have in mind here Plutarch's account of Cassius's Epicurean belief:

> '*In our sect, Brutus, we have an opinion that we do not always feel or see that which we suppose we do both see and feel; but that our senses being credulous, and therefore easily abused, when they are idle and unoccupied in their own objects, are induced to imagine they see and conjecture that which they in truth do not . . .*' (*Brutus*, pages 149–50).

276-301 *Art thou . . . Nor I, my lord.* Plutarch does not say that the ghost was that of Caesar, but Shakespeare makes it clear that it is both by the stage direction and the lines at V.5.17–19.

> *So Brutus boldly asked what he was, a god or a man, and what cause brought him thither. The spirit answered him: 'I am thy evil spirit, Brutus; and thou shalt see me by the city of Philippes.' Brutus, being no otherwise afraid, replied again unto it: 'Well, then I shall see thee again.' The spirit presently vanished away; and Brutus called his men unto him, who told him that they heard no noise, nor saw anything at all* (*Brutus*, page 149; see also *Caesar*, page 100).

276 *upon* toward
278 *stare* stand upright
281 *shalt* must
284 *will* am quite ready to
289 *false* out of tune

225

302   *commend me* deliver my greeting
303   *set on* advance
       betimes early in the morning

V.1.4   *proves* turns out to be
       battles troops in battle order
5   *warn* challenge
       at Philippi here. The meeting at Sardis actually took place at the beginning of 42 B.C., and the Battle of Philippi in the following autumn.
6   *Answering before we do demand of them* answering a call to battle before we have issued it
7   *in their bosoms* in their secret thoughts
8–9   *could be content | To visit other places* wish they were somewhere else
10   *With fearful bravery* with a show of splendour which conceals the fear they are feeling. Shakespeare took this detail from Plutarch: 'In truth, Brutus' army was inferior to Octavius Caesar's in number of men. But, for bravery and rich furniture, Brutus' army far excelled Caesar's. For the most part of their armours were silver and gilt, which Brutus had bountifully given them' (*Brutus*, page 151).
       face outward appearance
11   *fasten* fix the idea
13   *gallant* splendid. See note to line 10.
14   *bloody sign.* Plutarch has: 'The next morning, by break of day, the signal of battle was set out in Brutus' and Cassius' camp, which was an arming scarlet coat' (*Brutus*, page 154).
16   *battle* army
       softly slowly
18–20   *Upon the right . . . do so.* In Plutarch this disagreement about the leading of the wings takes place between Brutus and Cassius: 'Brutus prayed Cassius he might have the leading of the right wing, the which men

226

thought was far meeter for Cassius, both because he
was the elder man, and also for that he had the better
experience. But yet Cassius gave it him' (*Brutus*,
pages 155–6).

19 *exigent* emergency

20 *I do not cross you* I am not opposing you perversely
 will intend to

24 *answer on their charge* meet them when they attack

25 *Make forth* advance

27–66 *Words before ... stomachs.* This billingsgate before the
 battle is not in Plutarch, but was a common feature in
 Elizabethan drama.

33 *The posture of your blows* the nature of the blows
 you can produce. 'Posture' was a technical term referring to the position of a weapon in either arms drill or
 war.

34 *Hybla.* This is the name of a town and a mountain in
 Sicily which was proverbially famous for the quality of
 its honey. The reference by Cassius is to Antony's
 protestations of friendship after Caesar's death; Antony's reply refers only to his eloquence at the funeral
 and its results.

39 *so* (that is, threaten, and so give warning)

41 *showed your teeth* smiled insincerely
 fawned like hounds. See III.1.42–6.

47 *If Cassius might have ruled* (that is, if Cassius had had
 his way about their treatment of Antony after Caesar's
 death; see II.1.155–61).

48 *the cause* the matter in hand. The term is a legal one and
 this implication is taken up in 'proof' and 'arguing'.

49 *The proof* the trial or test

52 *goes up* will be sheathed

53 *three and thirty wounds.* All historical authorities, including Plutarch, have 'three and twenty'. The error
 may have been due to a misexpanded numeral in the
 manuscript.

54–5 *or till another Caesar | Have added slaughter to the sword*

        of traitors or until another Caesar (Octavius) shall have
been killed by traitors' swords

61   *peevish* silly, childish

        schoolboy. Octavius was actually twenty-one years old.

62   *a masquer and a reveller.* Plutarch notes in *Antonius* that
the Roman noblemen disapproved of Antony's

> *naughty life; for they did abhor his banquets and drun-*
> *ken feasts he made at unseasonable times, and his*
> *extreme wasteful expenses upon vain light huswives. . . .*
> *In his house they did nothing but feast, dance, and mask.*
> *And himself passed away the time in hearing of foolish*
> *plays, or in marrying these players, tumblers, jesters,*
> *and such sort of people* (page 183).

66   *stomachs* appetites, inclination (for battle)

68   *on the hazard* at stake. Originally this was a term from
gambling.

71   *as.* This was a common redundancy in phrases express-
ing time.

74   *As Pompey was.* At the Battle of Pharsalia, Pompey
was forced to fight Caesar against his better judgement.
Shakespeare is following Plutarch closely in this passage:

> *But touching Cassius, Messala reporteth that . . . after*
> *supper he took him by the hand, and holding him fast,*
> *in token of kindness as his manner was, told him in*
> *Greek: 'Messala, I protest unto thee, and make thee my*
> *witness, that I am compelled against my mind and will,*
> *as Pompey the Great was, to jeopard the liberty of our*
> *country to the hazard of a battle. And yet we must be*
> *lively and of good courage. . . .' Cassius having spoken*
> *these last words unto him, he bade him farewell and*
> *willed him to come to supper to him the next night*
> *following, because it was his birthday* (*Brutus*, pages
> 153–4).

    set stake, gamble

76   *held Epicurus strong* was a convinced follower of the philosophy of Epicurus. This postulated that since the gods were indifferent to the affairs of human beings, then omens and portents could have no significance. Plutarch speaks three times of Cassius's Epicureanism, and in connexion with the omens seen by the Republican armies notes that they 'began somewhat to alter Cassius' mind from Epicurus' opinions, and had put the soldiers also in a marvellous fear' (*Brutus*, page 152).

79–83   *Coming from ... gone.* This is based on Plutarch's *Brutus*: '. . . two eagles . . . lighted upon two of the foremost ensigns, and always followed the soldiers, which gave them meat, and fed them, until they came near to the city of Philippes; and there, one day only before the battle, they both flew away' (page 150).

79   *former* forward, foremost

84   *ravens, crows, and kites.* These were considered birds of ill-omen since they prognosticate death. This was probably suggested by Plutarch's 'a marvellous number of fowls of prey, that feed upon dead carcases' (*Brutus*, page 152).

86   *sickly* dying

87   *fatal* foreboding death

89   *but* only

91   *constantly* resolutely

92   *Even so, Lucilius.* Brutus has been talking aside to his aide while Cassius has been talking with Messala.

92–9   *Now, most noble Brutus ... to do?* This is a case of Shakespeare versifying what he found in Plutarch:

> *Cassius began to speak first, and said: 'The gods grant us, O Brutus, that this day we may win the field and ever after to live all the rest of our life quietly one with another. But sith the gods have so ordained it that the greatest and chiefest things amongst men are most uncertain, and that, if the battle fall out otherwise today than we wish or look for, we shall hardly meet again,*

> *what art thou then determined to do – to fly, or die?'*
> (*Brutus*, page 154).

93 *The gods today stand friendly.* May the gods stand friendly!

94 *Lovers* dear friends

95 *rests still* remain ever. The plural subject with the singular verb form is common in Shakespeare's grammar.

96 *Let's reason with the worst that may befall.* Let us consider what is to be done if the worst happens.

100–7 *Even by ... below.* Many editors have suggested that these lines are inconsistent with his next speech and with his suicide in V.5. However, Shakespeare is merely showing the philosopher at war with the soldier in Brutus. This is based closely on Plutarch:

> *Brutus answered him: '... I trust (I know not how) a certain rule of philosophy by the which I did greatly blame and reprove Cato for killing of himself, as being no lawful nor godly act, touching the gods, nor, concerning men, valiant; not to give place and yield to divine providence, and not constantly and patiently to take whatsoever it pleaseth him to send us, but to draw back and fly'* (*Brutus*, pages 154–5).

100 *that philosophy.* According to Plutarch, Brutus 'loved Plato's sect best' (*Brutus*, page 103).

101 *Cato.* This was Cato the Younger; see note to II.1.295.

104 *fall* happen

104–5 *to prevent | The time of life* to anticipate the natural limit of life

106 *stay* wait for
  providence fate, destiny
  some whatever. Brutus does not believe in the traditional Roman gods, merely some supernatural power.

108 *led in triumph.* Triumphs were not normally granted to

victories in civil wars, the exception being Caesar's
victory over Pompey's sons; see note to I.1.32–4.

109 *Thorough* archaic form of 'through'

110–18 *No, Cassius . . . well made.* Shakespeare is here following Plutarch closely:

> 'But being now in the midst of the danger, I am of a
> contrary mind. For, if it be not the will of God that this
> battle fall out fortunate for us, I will look no more for
> hope, neither seek to make any new supply for war
> again, but will rid me of this miserable world, and con-
> tent me with my fortune. For I gave up my life for my
> country in the Ides of March, for the which I shall live
> in another more glorious world' (*Brutus*, page 155).

119–21 *For ever . . . well made.* This is based on Plutarch:
'Cassius fell a-laughing to hear what he said, and em-
bracing him: "Come on then," said he, "let us go and
charge our enemies with this mind. For either we shall
conquer, or we shall not need to fear the conquerors" '
(*Brutus*, page 155).

122–3 *O, that a man might know | The end of this day's business
ere it come!* Compare *2 Henry IV*, III.1.45–6:

> *O God! that one might read the book of fate,*
> *And see the revolution of the times.*

V.2 (stage direction) *Alarum* (a signal calling to arms)
Enter Brutus and Messala. In the Folio text this stage
direction follows immediately after the *Exeunt* at the
end of Brutus's last speech. Thus Brutus and Messala,
who have just left the stage, immediately re-enter 'in
another part of the battlefield'.

1 *bills* written orders. Plutarch notes that 'Brutus, that
led the right wing, sent little bills to the colonels and
captains of private bands, in the which he wrote the
word of the battle' (*Brutus*, page 156).

2   *the other side* (Cassius's wing)
3   *set on* attack
4   *cold demeanour* lack of spirit in fighting
5   *push* assault
6   *them all* the whole army

V.3.1-4   *O, look, Titinius . . . from him.* This is based on Plutarch:

> *Furthermore, perceiving his footmen to give ground, he did what he could to keep them from flying, and took an ensign from one of the ensign-bearers that fled, and stuck it fast at his feet; although with much ado he could scant keep his own guard together. So Cassius himself was at length compelled to fly, with a few about him, unto a little hill from whence they might easily see what was done in all the plain* (Brutus, page 159).

1   *villains* (Cassius's own men)
2   *mine own* my own men
3   *Ensign* standard bearer
4   *it* the standard
5-8   *O Cassius . . . enclosed.* This is based on Plutarch:

> *Cassius . . . was marvellous angry to see how Brutus' men ran to give charge upon their enemies and tarried not for the word of the battle nor commandment to give charge; and it grieved him beside that, after he had overcome them, his men fell straight to spoil and were not careful to compass in the rest of the enemies behind. But with tarrying too long also, more than through the valiantness or foresight of the captains his enemies, Cassius found himself compassed in with the right wing of his enemies' army* (Brutus, pages 158-9).

6   *on* over
10   *tents* encampment
11   *far* farther

14–32 *Titinius, if thou lov'st me ... for joy.* This is based on
Plutarch:

> *he sent Titinnius, one of them that was with him, to go
> and know what they were. Brutus' horsemen saw him
> coming afar off, whom when they knew that he was one
> of Cassius' chiefest friends, they shouted out for joy;
> and they that were familiarly acquainted with him
> lighted from their horses, and went and embraced him.
> The rest compassed him in round about a-horseback,
> with songs of victory and great rushing of their harness,
> so that they made all the field ring again for joy (Brutus,
> page 159).*

19 *even with* as quick as

21 *My sight was ever thick.* 'Cassius himself saw nothing,
for his sight was very bad' (*Brutus*, page 159).
  thick dim
  Regard observe

22 *not'st* observest

25 *compass* full revolution

29 *make to* approach
  on the spur at a gallop

31 *light* dismount

32 *ta'en* captured

33–5 *Come down ... my face.* 'Cassius thinking indeed that
Titinnius was taken of the enemies, he then spake these
words: "Desiring too much to live, I have lived to see
one of my best friends taken, for my sake, before my
face" ' (*Brutus*, page 160).

36–50 *Come hither ... note of him.* Compare:

> *After that, he [Cassius] ... took Pindarus with him,
> one of his freed bondmen, whom he reserved ever for such
> a pinch, since the cursed battle of the Parthians. ... But
> then casting his clóak over his head and holding out his
> bare neck unto Pindarus, he gave him his head to be
> stricken off. So the head was found severed from the*

> *body. But after that time Pindarus was never seen more*
> (*Brutus*, page 160).

38   *swore thee* made thee swear

      saving of when I spared

40   *attempt* perform

42   *search* probe, penetrate

43   *Stand not* do not delay

      hilts. This plural form is common in Shakespeare.

46   *sword that killed thee.* Plutarch notes that 'he . . . slew himself with the same sword with the which he strake Caesar' (*Caesar*, page 99).

47   *so* in such circumstances as these

48   *my will* what I (rather than Cassius) had wished

51-3   *It is but change . . . by Antony.* Compare:

> *Brutus had conquered all on his side, and Cassius had lost all on the other side. For nothing undid them but that Brutus went not to help Cassius, thinking he had overcome them, as himself had done; and Cassius on the other side tarried not for Brutus, thinking he had been overthrown, as himself was* (*Brutus*, page 158).

51   *change* exchange of fortune

60   *O setting sun* (according to line 109 it is three o'clock)

64   *dews.* See note to II.1.266.

65   *Mistrust of my success hath done this deed.* Fear of the outcome of my mission is responsible for this action.

67   *Melancholy's child.* Melancholics (like Cassius) are prone to imagine evils which are non-existent.

68   *apt* easily impressed

71   *the mother* Melancholy (and, by transference, Cassius, its victim)

78   *Hie* hasten

80-90   *Why didst thou . . . heart.* The details here are taken from Plutarch:

Titinnius crowned with a garland of triumph ... came
before with great speed unto Cassius. But when he per-
ceived, by the cries and tears of his friends which tor-
mented themselves, the misfortune that had chanced to
his captain Cassius by mistaking, he drew out his sword,
cursing himself a thousand times that he had tarried so
long, and so slew himself presently in the field (*Brutus*,
page 161).

80   *brave* noble

84   *misconstrued* (accent on second syllable)

85   *hold thee* wait

88   *regarded* respected, highly esteemed

89   *By your leave, gods.* He asks permission to end his life
before the time allotted to him by the gods.

94–5   *O Julius Caesar, thou art mighty yet!* | *Thy spirit walks*
abroad. Compare II.1.167–70; III.1.270–75.

96   *proper* own ('own proper' is repetition for emphasis)

97   *where* whether

99–101   *The last of all the Romans, fare thee well!* | *It is impossible*
that ever Rome | *Should breed thy fellow.* In Plutarch
Brutus 'knew nothing of his death, till he came very
near to his camp. So when he was come thither, after
he had lamented the death of Cassius, calling him the
last of all the Romans, being unpossible that Rome
should ever breed again so noble and valiant a man as
he ...' (*Brutus*, page 161).

104–6   *and to Thasos send his body.* | *His funerals shall not be in*
our camp, | *Lest it discomfort us.* In Plutarch Brutus
'caused his body to be buried and sent it to the city of
Thassos, fearing lest his funerals within the camp
should cause great disorder' (pages 161–2). Thasos was
an island near Philippi. The Folio reading 'Tharsus'
(Tarsus) was the name of towns in Cicilia and Bithynia.

105   *funerals.* Usually Shakespeare uses the singular form,
but he adopts the plural here under the influence of
Plutarch.

106 *discomfort us* dishearten our soldiers

108 *Labeo and Flavius.* Plutarch identifies these characters among the friends of Brutus who were slain in battle before his eyes, of whom 'the one was his lieutenant and the other captain of the pioneers of his camp' (*Brutus*, page 169).

     battles forces

110 *second fight.* According to Plutarch the second battle occurred twenty days after the first; Shakespeare treats the two battles as one.

V.4 (stage direction) *Enter Brutus, Messala.* . . . The stage device being used here is similar to that at the first stage direction of V.2.

2–6 *What . . . Cato, ho !* Compare:

> There was the son of M. Cato slain, valiantly fighting amongst the lusty youths. For, notwithstanding that he was very weary and overharried, yet would he not therefore fly, but manfully fighting and laying about him, telling aloud his name and also his father's name, at length he was beaten down amongst many other dead bodies of his enemies which he had slain round about him (*Brutus*, page 167).

2 *What bastard doth not?* Who is of such base blood who does not do so?

4 *I am the son of Marcus Cato, ho!* Therefore he was the brother of Brutus's wife; see note to II.1.295.

7–8 *And I am Brutus, Marcus Brutus, I! | Brutus, my country's friend; know me for Brutus!* There is no speech prefix in the Folio text, which has *Luc.* before line 9. Plutarch makes it clear that it is Lucilius who impersonates Brutus in this scene (see note to lines 12–17). If this change in the speech prefix is made, and the exit of Brutus indicated at line 1, the action is clear.

12–17 *Yield, or thou diest . . . the General.* Compare:

> *Amongst them there was one of Brutus' friends called Lucilius, who seeing a troop of barbarous men making no reckoning of all men else they met in their way, but going all together right against Brutus, he determined to stay them with the hazard of his life, and, being left behind, told them that he was Brutus; and, because they should believe him, he prayed them to bring him to Antonius.... These barbarous men being very glad of this good hap, and thinking themselves happy men, they carried him in the night, and sent some before unto Antonius to tell him of their coming. He was marvellous glad of it, and went out to meet them that brought him (Brutus, pages 167–8).*

12   *Only I yield to die.* I surrender simply in order to die.

13–14   *There is so much that thou wilt kill me straight: | Kill Brutus, and be honoured in his death.* Many editors add a stage direction after these lines indicating that Lucilius offers his captors a sum of money to kill him. This is not necessary as the meaning is 'There is so much inducement that you will surely kill me at once, and in doing so win great honour.'

13   *straight* immediately

15   *We must not* (perhaps because noble prisoners could be ransomed)

     (stage direction) *Enter Antony.* This is the position of Antony's entry in the Folio text. It is possible that it was placed here in the manuscript as an early warning for the prompter; however, it is more likely to indicate that Antony enters and is crossing the stage to where Lucilius and the soldiers stand, before the first soldier sees him and says line 17.

18–25   *Brutus is ta'en ... like himself.* Shakespeare is here following Plutarch very closely:

> *Lucilius was brought to him, who stoutly with a bold countenance said: 'Antonius, I dare assure thee that no enemy hath taken nor shall take Marcus Brutus alive.*

237

> *I beseech God keep him from that fortune. For where-*
> *soever he be found, alive or dead, he will be found like*
> *himself' (Brutus,* page 168).

25   *like himself* true to his own noble nature

26-9   *This is not . . . enemies.* Shakespeare follows Plutarch closely in these lines:

> *Antonius . . . looking upon all them that had brought*
> *him, said unto them: 'My companions, I think ye are*
> *sorry you have failed of your purpose, and that you*
> *think this man hath done you great wrong. But, I do*
> *assure you, you have taken a better booty than that you*
> *followed. For, instead of an enemy, you have brought*
> *me a friend. . . . For I had rather have such men my*
> *friends as this man here, than enemies.' Then he em-*
> *braced Lucilius and at that time delivered him to one of*
> *his friends in custody (Brutus,* pages 168-9).

30   *where* whether

32   *is chanced* has happened

V.5.1   *poor remains* pitiful survivors

2   *showed the torch-light.* The explanation of this line is found in Plutarch, but not in the play:

> *Furthermore, Brutus thought that there was no great*
> *number of men slain in battle; and, to know the truth*
> *of it, there was one called Statilius that promised to go*
> *through his enemies, for otherwise it was impossible to*
> *go see their camp, and from thence, if all were well, that*
> *he would lift up a torch-light in the air, and then return*
> *again with speed to him. The torch-light was lift up as*
> *he had promised, for Statilius went thither. Now Brutus*
> *seeing Statilius tarry long after that, and that he came*
> *not again, he said: 'If Statilius be alive, he will come*
> *again.' But his evil fortune was such that as he came*
> *back he lighted in his enemies' hands and was slain*
> *(Brutus,* page 170).

4-14   *Sit thee down . . . at his eyes.* 'Now, the night being far spent, Brutus as he sat bowed towards Clitus one of his men and told him somewhat in his ear, the other answered him not, but fell a-weeping. Thereupon he proved Dardanus, and said somewhat also to him' (*Brutus*, page 170).

5   *a deed in fashion.* The reference is to Cassius's suicide at V.3.

17   *The ghost of Caesar hath appeared to me.* This is based on Plutarch's *Caesar*: 'The second battle being at hand, this spirit appeared again unto him, but spake never a word. Thereupon Brutus, knowing he should die, did put himself to all hazard in battle' (pages 100–101).

18   *several* different

21-8   *Nay, I am sure . . . run on it.* 'At length he came to Volumnius himself, and, speaking to him in Greek, prayed him, for the study's sake which brought them acquainted together, that he would help him to put his hand to his sword, to thrust it in him to kill him. Volumnius denied his request' (*Brutus*, page 170).

22   *the world . . . how it goes* how things are

23   *the pit* the hole into which animals are driven (but also by a quibble 'the grave')

24   *more worthy* nobler

28   *sword-hilts.* See note to V.3.43.

30   *Fly, fly, my lord, there is no tarrying here.* 'And, amongst the rest, one of them said, there was no tarrying for them there, but that they must needs fly. Then Brutus rising up: "We must fly indeed," said he, "but it must be with our hands not with our feet" ' (*Brutus*, pages 170–71).

31-9   *Farewell to you . . . at once.* Shakespeare follows Plutarch closely in these lines:

> *Then, taking every man by the hand, he said these words unto them with a cheerful countenance : 'It rejoiceth my heart that not one of my friends hath failed me at my need, and I do not complain of my fortune, but only for*

239

> *my country's sake. For, as for me, I think myself happier*
> *than they that have overcome, considering that I leave*
> *a perpetual fame of our courage and manhood, the which*
> *our enemies the conquerors shall never attain unto by*
> *force nor money . . .' (Brutus, page 171).*

32   *asleep.* Strato does not therefore know what has passed
        between Brutus and Clito, Dardanius and Volumnius.

38   *vile conquest.* Brutus thus dies still believing that
        Caesar's death was necessary; and that the victory by
        Antony and Octavius means the end of Rome's free-
        dom, and is therefore 'vile'.

39   *at once* without further ado

42   *this hour* the hour of his death. This is in accord with
        Brutus's Stoic belief that death is not a calamity.

44–51   *I prithee . . . good a will.* Compare:

> . . . *he went a little aside with two or three only, among*
> *the which Strato was one. . . . He came as near to him*
> *as he could, and, taking his sword by the hilts with both*
> *his hands and falling down upon the point of it, ran*
> *himself through. Others say that not he, but Strato, at*
> *his request, held the sword in his hand, and turned his*
> *head aside, and that Brutus fell down upon it ; and so*
> *ran himself through, and died presently (Brutus, pages*
> 171–2).

45   *of a good respect* of good reputation

46   *smatch* taste, tincture

50   *Caesar, now be still.* In accordance with the revenge
        code, Caesar having now been avenged, his ghost can
        rest peacefully.

51   (stage direction) *Retreat.* This was a military term for
        a sounding of the recall by trumpets of a pursuing force.

52–4   *What man . . . Messala.* 'Messala, that had been Brutus'
        great friend, became afterwards Octavius Caesar's
        friend. So, shortly after, Caesar being at good leisure,

he brought Strato, Brutus' friend, unto him ...' (*Brutus*, page 172).

53   *My master's man.* In Plutarch, Strato was a fellow-student of Brutus's when he studied rhetoric.

55   *can but make a fire of him* can only put his corpse on a funeral pyre

59   *Lucilius' saying.* See V.4.21–2.

60   *entertain* take into service

62   *prefer* recommend

66   *follow* serve

67   *That did the latest service to my master.* In Plutarch, Messala introduces Strato to Octavius with ' "Caesar, behold, here is he that did the last service to my Brutus" ' (*Brutus*, page 172).

68–72   *This was the noblest Roman of them all ... one of them.* Compare:

> ... *Antonius spake it openly divers times that he thought that of all them that had slain Caesar there was none but Brutus only that was moved to do it as thinking the act commendable of itself; but that all the other conspirators did conspire his death for some private malice or envy that they otherwise did bear unto him* (*Brutus*, page 140).

71–2   *in a general honest thought | And common good to all* moved by a sincere belief that what he was doing was for the public good. Compare II.1.10–12.

73–5   *His life ... man.* This sums up admirably the whole impression given of Brutus by Plutarch throughout his *Brutus* by such remarks as 'he was a marvellous lowly and gentle person ... was well-beloved of the people ... was rightly made and framed unto virtue'.

73   *gentle* noble and magnanimous
     elements. The four elements (earth, air, fire, water) formed the humours of the body (phlegm, blood, melancholy, choler); all had to be in perfect balance for physical and spiritual health.

76   *use* treat

77   *respect* estimation, regard

       burial. Shakespeare took this word from Plutarch; although he did know the Roman practice of cremation; see line 55 and III.2.255.

79   *ordered honourably* treated with all honour. Shakespeare transfers Antony's action in Plutarch to Octavius: 'Antonius having found Brutus' body, he caused it to be wrapped up in one of the richest coat-armours he had' (*Brutus*, page 172).

81   *part* divide

AN ACCOUNT OF THE TEXT

The Tragedy of Julius Caesar was first printed in the Folio edition of Shakespeare's plays of 1623. The copy the printers used was probably a transcript of some kind rather than Shakespeare's own manuscript, as there is an absence of typical Shakespeare spellings such as appear in other texts printed from authorial copy. The manuscript may well have been one that had been used as a prompt book, because some of the stage directions appear to be theatrical in character. The Folio text is the only early printed version of the play which has any authority; the texts found in the later Folios of 1632, 1664, and 1685, and in the six seventeenth-century quarto editions, are all ultimately based on the first printing.

In general the text is a good one, the only errors being a few typographical misprints, occasional mispunctuation, some mislineation due to the requirements of spacing on the Folio page, some wrong assignment of speeches, and some verbal corruptions. The origin of most of the readings that are obviously or probably incorrect is susceptible of satisfactory explanation.

But there is some evidence that the play underwent a certain amount of revision between its composition and its first appearance in print. Two passages convincingly support this hypothesis. The first is at III.1.47–8, which reads:

> *Know, Caesar doth not wrong, nor without cause*
> *Will he be satisfied.*

This was apparently not the original and acted version of the lines, for Ben Jonson, in his *Timber: Or Discoveries Made Upon Men and Matters*, notes about Shakespeare:

> *Many times he fell into those things, could not escape laughter:*
> *as when he said in the person of Caesar, one speaking to him,*

> Caesar thou dost me wrong; *he replied,* Caesar did never wrong, but with just cause; *and such like, which were ridiculous.*

In his the *Staple of News* also, Jonson makes fun of the same lines:

EXPECTATION I can do that too, if I have cause.
PROLOGUE Cry you mercy, *you never did wrong, but with just cause.*

It would seem probable, therefore, that the Folio text represents an adjustment of the original lines made by Shakespeare or his theatre company in response to Jonson's criticism.

The second passage occurs in IV.3.145–93, where there are two contradictory accounts of Portia's death. The first of these, at lines 145–56, shows Brutus in part accounting for his loss of temper with the intruding poet by informing Cassius of his grief at having heard the news that Portia has committed suicide, and thus reinforces our impression of Brutus as a very human though publicly dedicated man. In the second account, at lines 179–93, Brutus denies he has had word from Rome concerning his wife, and on being informed of her death by Messala, accepts the news with a display of superhuman fortitude:

> *Why, farewell, Portia. We must die, Messala.*
> *With meditating that she must die once,*
> *I have the patience to endure it now. . . .*
> *Well, to our work alive.*

Although some critics have defended the presence of these two passages, it is generally believed that the version at lines 145–56 was a later addition intended to replace the exchange at lines 179–93, which was imperfectly deleted in the manuscript from which the Folio text was printed. If lines 179–93 are omitted, the scene runs quite smoothly with Brutus's line 'Well, to our work alive' referring to Cicero's death, which is announced by Messala in lines 177–8, instead of to Portia's.

Other evidence of revision or cutting, which have been adduced by various scholars, and which carry less conviction than those already mentioned, are: the appearance of Publius at

Caesar's house in II.2 in place of Cassius who declares, at
II.1.212, that he intends to join the other conspirators in bring-
ing Caesar to the Capitol; and some inconsistencies seen in the
behaviour of Casca, which have led to the contention that he is a
'ragbag' character formed from the conflating of previously
separate roles.

COLLATIONS

1

Below are listed departures in the present text of *Julius Caesar*
from that of the First Folio, whose reading is given on the right
of the square bracket. Most of these emendations were first
made by eighteenth-century editors of the play. Those found in
one of the three seventeenth-century reprints of the Folio (F2,
F3, and F4) are indicated.

I.1.   22   tradesman's] Tradesmans
            women's] womens
       37   Pompey? Many a time and oft] Pompey many a
            time and oft?
       39   windows, yea,] Windowes? Yea,
I.2. 127   'Alas!'] (*It is not clear from F1 whether* Alas *is part
            of Caesar's reported speech, or Cassius's comment
            on it.*)
      154   walls] Walkes
      165   not – so with] not so (with
      242   hooted] howted
      246   swooned] swoonded
      249   swoon] swound
      252   like; he] like he
I.3.   28   Hooting] Howting
      129   In favour's like] Is Fauors, like
II.1. 15   Crown him! – that!] Crowne him that
       23   climber-upward] Climber upward
       40   ides] first

II.1.   52   What, Rome?] What Rome?

       67   of man] (F2); of a man

       83   path, thy] path thy

     246   wafture] wafter

     295   reputed, Cato's] reputed: Cato's

     330   going] going,

II.2.   19   fought] fight

      23   did neigh] (F2); do neigh

      46   are] heare

III.1.   39   law] lane

    113   states] (F2); state

    115   lies] (F2); lye

    209   strucken] stroken

    283   catching, for] (F2); catching from

III.2. 105   art] (F2); are

    111   Has he, masters?] Ha's hee Masters?

    158   will?] Will:

  204–6   SECOND PLEBEIAN We will be revenged. | ALL Revenge!... live.] 2. We will be reueng'd: Reueng | About... slay, | Let... liue.

    222   wit] (F2); writ

IV.2.   13   Lucilius;] Lucillius

     14   you,] you:

     50   Lucius] Lucilius

     52   Lucilius] Let Lucius

IV.3. 4–5   letters, praying ... man, was] Letters, praying ... man was

    227   say?] say.

    229   (stage direction) *Enter Lucius*] (*In F1 this follows hence (line 228 of this edition*).)

V.1.   41   teeth] (F3); teethes

     69   (stage direction) *Lucilius stands forth, and talks with Brutus apart*] Lucillius and Messala stand forth. (*In F1 this follows* with you (*line 69 of this edition*).)

    109   Rome?] Rome.

V.3.   97   have not crowned] (*Some copies of F1 have:* haue crown'd.)

V.3. 101   more tears] mo teares (*Some copies of F1 have:* no teares.)

104   Thasos] Tharsus

V.4. 7–8 LUCILIUS] (*F1 has no speech prefix.*)

9   O] *Luc.* O

17   the news] thee news

V.5. 23   (stage direction) *Low alarums*] (*Some copies of F1 have :* Loud Alarums.)

33   to thee too, Strato. Countrymen] to thee, to Strato, Countrymen:

40   life's] liues

71   He only,] (F2); He, onely

2

Below are listed instances where the present text of *Julius Caesar* preserves readings of the First Folio (modernized according to the principles of this edition) that have often, with some plausibility, been amended. Emendations found in some editions of the play are given after the square bracket.

I.1. 15 FLAVIUS] MARULLUS

22   tradesman's] (F1 Tradesmans); tradesmen's; trade, – man's; trades, man's

    women's] (F1 womens); woman's

23   withal I] with all. I; with awl. I

61   where] whe're; whe'r; whether

I.2. 72   laughter] laugher; lover; talker

87   both] death

123   bend] beam

159   eternal] infernal

187   senators] senator

242   hooted] (F1 howted); shouted

246   swooned] (F1 swoonded); swounded

252   like; he] (F1 like he); like, he

I.3. 21   glazed] gazed; glared

I.3. 65 old men, fools] old men fool
129 In favour's like] (F1 Is Fauors, like); Is favoured
like; Is feav'rous like; It favours like

II.1. 15 Crown him! – that!] (F1 Crowne him that); Crown
him? – that –
83 path, thy] (F1 path thy); march, thy; put thy;
pass thy; hath thy
114 not the face] that the face; that the fate; not the
faiths; not the faith
255 know you Brutus] know you, Brutus
279 gentle Brutus] gentle, Brutus
295 reputed, Cato's] (F1 reputed: Cato's); reputed
Cato's

II.2. 19 fought] (F1 fight); did fight
46 are] (F1 heare); were
81 And] Of
129 earns] yearns

III.1. 21 or] on
39 law] (F1 lane); line; play; lune
101 CASCA] CASSIUS
105–10 Stoop . . . liberty!] (*Some editors give these lines to
Casca.*)
114 BRUTUS] CASCA
116 CASSIUS] BRUTUS
174 in strength of malice] exempt from malice; no
strength of malice; in strength of amity; in strength
of welcome; forspent of malice; in strength of
friendship; in strength of manhood; unfraught of
malice
206 lethe] death
209 strucken] (F1 stroken); stricken
258 hand] hands
262 limbs] line; loins; lives; times; minds; kind;
tombs; souls; heads; bonds
285 Began] Begin

III.2. 71 blest] most blest
111 Has he, masters?] (F1 Ha's hee Masters?); Has he,

248

		my master?; Has he not, masters?; That he has, masters.; That has he, masters.
III.2.	250	this] that
III.3.	2	unluckily] unlucky; unlikely
IV.1.	37	objects, arts] abject orts; abjects, orts; abject arts
	44	our means stretched] and our best means stretched out; our means stretched to the utmost; our means, our plans stretched out; our choicest means stretched out; all our means stretched
IV.3.	4–5	letters, praying . . . man, was] (F1 Letters, praying . . . man was); letter, praying . . . man, was; letter (praying . . . man) was; letters, praying . . . man, were
	13	speaks] speak
	27	bay] bait
	28	bait] bay
	54	noble] able
	108	humour] honour
	109	lamb] man; temper; heart
	207	new-added] (F1 new added); new aided; new-hearted
V.1.	105	time] term
	106	some] those
V.3.	97	where] whether; whe'r; if
	99	The last] Thou last
	104	Thasos] (F1 Tharsus); Thassos
V.4.	7–8	LUCILIUS] (*F1 has no speech prefix*); BRUTUS
	30	where] whe'r; whether; if

3

In the present edition of *Julius Caesar* some of the stage directions printed in the First Folio have been expanded. Also directions for stage action clearly required by the text have been added. The following list records in square brackets the more important additional directions, and those words introduced into the directions of the Folio.

I.2.   o   *Enter ... Antony, [stripped] for the course, ... [and a great crowd]*

I.3.   o   *Enter Casca and Cicero [, meeting]*

II.1.   60   *[Exit Lucius]*

       76   *[Exit Lucius]*

     100   *They whisper [apart]*

     191   *[A] clock strikes*

     228   *Exeunt [the conspirators]*

     303   *Knock[ing]*

     321   *[He throws off the kerchief]*

II.2. 124   TREBONIUS *Caesar, I will. [Aside] And so near ...*

II.3.   o   *Enter Artemidorus [reading a paper]*

III.1.   o   *Enter Caesar ... [Popilius,] ...*

      12   *[Caesar enters the Capitol, the rest following]*

      14   *[He goes to speak to Caesar]*

      26   *[Exeunt Antony and Trebonius]*

III.2.   o   *Enter Brutus and [later] goes into the pulpit ...*

      10   *[Exit Cassius, with some of the Plebeians]*

      40   *Enter Mark Antony [and others], ...*

     162   *[Antony comes down from the pulpit]*

     198   *[Antony plucks off the mantle]*

     261   *Exeunt Plebeians [with the body]* (F1: *Exit Plebeians*)

III.3.   4   *[The Plebeians surround him]*

      35   *[They attack Cinna]*

      38   *Exeunt all the Plebeians [with Cinna's body]*

IV.2.   o   *Enter Brutus, Lucilius, [Lucius,] ...*

      13   *[Brutus and Lucilius draw apart]*

      52   *Exeunt [all except Brutus and Cassius]* (F1: *Manet Brutus and Cassius*)

IV.3. 122   *Enter a Poet [followed by Lucius; Titinius and Lucilius attempting to restrain him]*

     140   *[Exeunt Lucilius and Titinius]*
            [Exit Lucius]

     155   *Enter Boy [Lucius]*

     160   *[Exit Lucius] [Cassius drinks]*

     229   *[Exit Lucius]*

     236   *Exeunt [Cassius, Titinius, and Messala]*

IV.3. 249 *[Varro and Claudius lie down]*
    264 *[Lucius falls asleep]*
    272 *[He sits and reads]*
    284 *[Exit Ghost]*
V.1.   20 *Enter Brutus . . . [Lucilius, Titinius, Messala, and others]*
    69 *[Lucilius stands forth, and talks with Brutus apart]*
    70 *[Messala stands forth]*
    92 *[Brutus rejoins Cassius]*
V.3.   22 *[Pindarus ascends]*
    25 *[To Pindarus]*
    35 *Enter Pindarus [from above]*
    46 *[He dies]*
    50 *[Exit]*
    79 *[Exit Messala]*
    90 *Enter Brutus . . . Volumnius, [Labeo, Flavius,] . . .*
V.4.   0 *Enter Brutus, Messala, [Young] Cato . . .*
    1 *[Exit, followed by Messala and Flavius]*
    8 *[Young Cato is slain]*
V.5.   5 *[He whispers]*
    8 *[He whispers]*
    43 *[Exeunt Clitus, Dardanius, and Volumnius]*

READ MORE IN PENGUIN

In every corner of the world, on every subject under the sun, Penguin represents quality and variety – the very best in publishing today.

For complete information about books available from Penguin – including Puffins, Penguin Classics and Arkana – and how to order them, write to us at the appropriate address below. Please note that for copyright reasons the selection of books varies from country to country.

In the United Kingdom: Please write to *Dept. EP, Penguin Books Ltd, Bath Road, Harmondsworth, West Drayton, Middlesex UB7 0DA*

In the United States: Please write to *Consumer Sales, Penguin USA, P.O. Box 999, Dept. 17109, Bergenfield, New Jersey 07621-0120*. VISA and MasterCard holders call 1-800-253-6476 to order Penguin titles

In Canada: Please write to *Penguin Books Canada Ltd, 10 Alcorn Avenue, Suite 300, Toronto, Ontario M4V 3B2*

In Australia: Please write to *Penguin Books Australia Ltd, P.O. Box 257, Ringwood, Victoria 3134*

In New Zealand: Please write to *Penguin Books (NZ) Ltd, Private Bag 102902, North Shore Mail Centre, Auckland 10*

In India: Please write to *Penguin Books India Pvt Ltd, 706 Eros Apartments, 56 Nehru Place, New Delhi 110 019*

In the Netherlands: Please write to *Penguin Books Netherlands bv, Postbus 3507, NL-1001 AH Amsterdam*

In Germany: Please write to *Penguin Books Deutschland GmbH, Metzlerstrasse 26, 60594 Frankfurt am Main*

In Spain: Please write to *Penguin Books S. A., Bravo Murillo 19, 1° B, 28015 Madrid*

In Italy: Please write to *Penguin Italia s.r.l., Via Felice Casati 20, I-20124 Milano*

In France: Please write to *Penguin France S. A., 17 rue Lejeune, F-31000 Toulouse*

In Japan: Please write to *Penguin Books Japan, Ishikiribashi Building, 2-5-4, Suido, Bunkyo-ku, Tokyo 112*

In South Africa: Please write to *Longman Penguin Southern Africa (Pty) Ltd, Private Bag X08, Bertsham 2013*

RSC
ROYAL
SHAKESPEARE
COMPANY

The Royal Shakespeare Company today is probably one of the best known theatre companies in the world, playing regularly to audiences of more than a million people a year. The RSC has three theatres in Stratford-upon-Avon, the Royal Shakespeare Theatre, the Swan Theatre and The Other Place, and two theatres in London's Barbican Centre, the Barbican Theatre and The Pit. The Company also has an annual season in Newcastle-upon-Tyne and regularly undertakes tours throughout the UK and overseas.

Find out more about the RSC and its current repertoire by joining the Company's mailing list. Not only will you receive advance information of all the Company's activities, but also priority booking, special ticket offers, copies of the RSC Magazine and special offers on RSC publications and merchandise.

If you would like to receive details of the Company's work and an application form for the mailing list please write to:

RSC Membership Office
Royal Shakespeare Theatre
FREEPOST
Stratford-upon-Avon
CV37 6BR

or telephone: 01789 205301

READ MORE IN PENGUIN

CRITICAL STUDIES

Described by *The Times Educational Supplement* as 'admirable' and 'superb', Penguin Critical Studies is a specially developed series of critical essays on the major works of literature for use by students in universities, colleges and schools.

Titles published or in preparation include:

READ MORE IN PENGUIN

THE NEW PENGUIN SHAKESPEARE

All's Well That Ends Well	Barbara Everett
Antony and Cleopatra	Emrys Jones
As You Like It	H. J. Oliver
The Comedy of Errors	Stanley Wells
Coriolanus	G. R. Hibbard
Hamlet	T. J. B. Spencer
Henry IV, Part 1	P. H. Davison
Henry IV, Part 2	P. H. Davison
Henry V	A. R. Humphreys
Henry VI, Parts 1–3	Norman Sanders
(three volumes)	
Henry VIII	A. R. Humphreys
Julius Caesar	Norman Sanders
King John	R. L. Smallwood
King Lear	G. K. Hunter
Love's Labour's Lost	John Kerrigan
Macbeth	G. K. Hunter
Measure for Measure	J. M. Nosworthy
The Merchant of Venice	W. Moelwyn Merchant
The Merry Wives of Windsor	G. R. Hibbard
A Midsummer Night's Dream	Stanley Wells
Much Ado About Nothing	R. A. Foakes
The Narrative Poems	Maurice Evans
Othello	Kenneth Muir
Pericles	Philip Edwards
Richard II	Stanley Wells
Richard III	E. A. J. Honigmann
Romeo and Juliet	T. J. B. Spencer
The Sonnets *and* A Lover's Complaint	John Kerrigan
The Taming of the Shrew	G. R. Hibbard
The Tempest	Anne Barton
Timon of Athens	G. R. Hibbard
Troilus and Cressida	R. A. Foakes
Twelfth Night	M. M. Mahood
The Two Gentlemen of Verona	Norman Sanders
The Two Noble Kinsmen	N. W. Bawcutt
The Winter's Tale	Ernest Schanzer